S. HRG. 114–689

REGIONAL IMPACT OF THE SYRIA CONFLICT: SYRIA, TURKEY AND IRAQ

HEARING

BEFORE THE

COMMITTEE ON FOREIGN RELATIONS
UNITED STATES SENATE

ONE HUNDRED FOURTEENTH CONGRESS

SECOND SESSION

SEPTEMBER 29, 2016

Printed for the use of the Committee on Foreign Relations

Available via the World Wide Web:
http://www.fdsys.gpo.gov

U.S. GOVERNMENT PUBLISHING OFFICE

26–911 PDF   WASHINGTON : 2017

For sale by the Superintendent of Documents, U.S. Government Publishing Office
Internet: bookstore.gpo.gov   Phone: toll free (866) 512–1800; DC area (202) 512–1800
Fax: (202) 512–2104   Mail: Stop IDCC, Washington, DC 20402–0001

CONTENTS

(III)

REGIONAL IMPACT OF THE SYRIA CONFLICT: SYRIA, TURKEY AND IRAQ

THURSDAY, SEPTEMBER 29, 2016

U.S. SENATE,
COMMITTEE ON FOREIGN RELATIONS,
Washington, DC.

The committee met, pursuant to notice, at 10:00 a.m. in Room SD–419, Dirksen Senate Office Building, Hon. Bob Corker, chairman of the committee, presiding.

Present: Senators Corker [presiding], Rubio, Isakson, Cardin, Menendez, Shaheen, Murphy, and Markey.

OPENING STATEMENT OF HON. BOB CORKER, U.S. SENATOR FROM TENNESSEE

The CHAIRMAN. The Senate Foreign Relations Committee will come to order.

We welcome our Deputy Secretary of State, Tony Blinken. I know he was in Turkey until yesterday evening, and we moved the hearing back a day.

I would note that we have been trying to get Secretary Kerry in here for some time. That has not been possible. I do not want to diminish your appearance, because we are thankful to have you here. But I think for obvious reasons, he has not been willing to come.

I think the focus of today's hearing will be Syria. I do not think anyone here can be proud of the United States' role in the greatest humanitarian disaster of our time and what we have done to enable that to happen.

As I think about your appearance here today, I think in many ways it will be helpful to us as we think about the next administration, the next Secretary of State, the relationship that needs to exist between the executive branch and the Secretary of State's office. I know that you came over from the National Security staff, so you were at the White House. Then you moved to the State Department. I know sometimes executive branch folks like to have their own people at the State Department, and I know, for instance, you were to appear here yesterday but the President ordered you to Turkey instead. So it speaks to sort of the overlap that sometimes exists between the executive branch and the Department of State.

As an observation, the entire Syrian conflict is again something that we are not proud of. I do not think anybody here is proud of it. Even though I think they would view the Obama administration's foreign policy, generally speaking, as a failure, It is inter-

(1)

esting that Secretary Clinton has received support from the foreign policy establishment because I think it is so well known that she tried to counter so much of what happened and what has lessened our standing in the world. And I think that is the reason that many people have migrated in the foreign policy establishment to her and are now supporting her. I think all of us are aware of her trying to counter what happened in Iraq, trying to do more to support the rebels. I think that is just widely known.

What is interesting to me, is Secretary Kerry. He came in with a lot of excitement. I mean, people thought he lived his whole life, if you will, to be Secretary of State. Even as a young person, he was involved in foreign policy. He fought in Vietnam and made his name, if you will, on the stage here as a young man. But after what has happened in Syria and what happened in Iraq, that moved—feelings by many—certainly by me—to anger. To now, we had a breakfast with him just a week and a half ago, and to me he has become a somewhat sympathetic figure in that he is out there trying to deal with, for instance, the situation in Syria. And yet there is no Plan B. There is no support from the White House.

We have had General Allen here—we knew in March of 2015— who was on Secretary Kerry's behalf working hard to create a no-fly zone, and talking openly about it. Turkey was supporting that. And yet there was no decision from the White House.

The clearest example of why our foreign policy has been such a failure was this weekend. Ben and I were trying to set up a meeting to try to deal with the issue of JASTA, to try to come to some other option that might create an outlet for the victims of 9/11 and yet not undermine some of our sovereign immunity issues. I know I have been talking to the White House for some time just trying to get them to engage with us. Over the weekend, I talked to Secretary Kerry twice, and we agreed the best way to resolve this was to have a meeting, a meeting with Chuck Schumer, a meeting with John Cornyn, a meeting with Ben and myself, a meeting with Senator Reid and Senator McConnell. Just to sit down and see if another option could be developed that might cause us to move in a direction that would create an outlet for the people of 9/11 and yet not to have some of the adverse consequences that some of us fear.

Secretary Kerry could not even get the White House to call a meeting. Let me say that one more time. The outburst yesterday from the White House over what happened is remarkable when they would not even sit down to meet with the Secretary of State and members of the Senate to try to create a solution to a problem that they felt was real.

So I have to tell you—I know all of you guys write books after you leave. I think it is going to be a fascinating walk through what I believe to be a failed presidency as it relates to foreign policy. There has been an unwillingness to roll up sleeves and deal with tough issues, and certainly there is no way to deal with them without conversation—and then to not have a Plan B, where the diplomatic actions cannot be backed up because Russia and Assad realize that there is no Plan B. Never has been a Plan B.

So I look forward to your testimony. I know I am being a little tough on you today, but I think it is in response to just seeing again why this failure has occurred, and that is the White House's inability to sit down, to get involved, to be willing to put forth tough consequences when things do not occur. Again, there could not be more evidence of that than the unwillingness to even sit down and try to propose another way of dealing with the situation we dealt with yesterday on the Senate floor.

So with that, I turn to my good friend, Senator Cardin, and look forward to his opening comments.

STATEMENT OF HON. BENJAMIN L. CARDIN, U.S. SENATOR FROM MARYLAND

Senator CARDIN. Well, thank you, Mr. Chairman.

Secretary Blinken, thank you for being here.

Chairman Corker and I have been partners during most of this Congress on this committee, and we share very similar views about foreign policy and priorities. And we have had an opportunity to work together on many, many issues.

As I was listening to Senator Corker, at the beginning of his comments, I thought we were going to be able to continue that with his nice comments about Secretary Clinton because I share those views on Secretary Clinton's extraordinary talent to conduct foreign policy.

And I share Senator Corker's frustration on JASTA. I think that was highlighted through circumstances that neither he nor I could control, nor could the administration control, and that is, that the timing of JASTA required us to take the veto override before the recess. I think if we could have had that veto override during the lame duck session, we would have had more opportunity to explore ways in which we could try to accomplish the needed removal of sovereign immunity that stands in the path of the victims of 9/11 but do it in a way that does not cause the risk factors that this legislation causes.

And neither Senator Corker nor I and, quite frankly, the leadership or the President could affect that timing because the President had to act with a certain number of days, the Congress was required to take up the veto message immediately unless we had unanimous consent, which was unlikely to be able to be gotten. So I think it put us in a position where options were not as robust as I would have liked them to have been and that included the President's option.

So I am not as critical as Senator Corker of this administration or Secretary Kerry. I know Secretary Kerry felt pretty passionately about the JASTA legislation. He expressed his views. I had a chance to be with Secretary Kerry on a plane for a considerable period of time, and he used that opportunity to explore every opportunity we had here to deal with JASTA. So I very much admire Secretary Kerry's optimism and his unrelenting pursuit of peace in every part of the world. And we had a chance to experience that firsthand in Colombia, as we saw after 5 decades of civil war, a peace agreement signed this past Monday, and I was proud to be there with Secretary Kerry.

Secretary Blinken, welcome back to the Senate Foreign Relations Committee. It is not every day that we have a star from Sesame Street with us. For anyone who has not seen Secretary Blinken's guest appearance with Grover, I encourage you to watch him discuss refugees with everyone's favorite furry blue monster before the President's summit on refugees during the U.N. General Assembly session.

We know that you have just returned from a trip to Turkey, and we look forward to learning about your discussions there given Turkey's critical role in the success of a counter-ISIL campaign, ending the conflict in Syria, and for broader regional ability.

Charged with oversight of the State Department, the members of this committee have a fundamental interest in the success of U.S. diplomacy and U.S. leadership in the foreign policy arena. Secretary Kerry is correct in his belief that the tools of diplomacy should always be the preferred method for stopping violence, saving lives, and restoring stability.

I want to commend the dedication of Secretary Kerry and yourself and our Nation's diplomats for the work you have done around the clock with both allies and adversaries to forge an agreement to end violence in Syria. That is what we need to do. There is no way to end that civil war through the use of military force. We need to be able to have a negotiated diplomatic solution where all sides respect a government that respects human rights.

But now we are clearly at an inflection point. The U.S.-Russia ceasefire agreement was based on the assumption that Russia could compel the Assad regime to ground its air force, that Russia would compel the Assad regime to allow immediate and unfettered humanitarian access. We have clearly seen that neither of these two objectives were achieved.

Russia strives to be considered a peer, one that is essential to solving global problems, but I seriously question the reliability of Russia in this regard. We must reevaluate our approach to Russia in the Middle East and beyond the Middle East. Russia continues to attack Ukraine forces in Donbass. It illegally occupies Crimea. It has hacked into our computer system and sought to destabilize our electoral process. These are not the actions of a partner. These are the actions of an adversary, and I think we have to recognize that.

With our focus on Russia, we cannot lose sight of Iran's nefarious role in Syria and beyond. We know that Iran is backing the Assad regime economically and militarily. IRGC commanders have died fighting in Syria. Iran has mobilized militia fighters, provided intelligence to support Syria and Russia in targeting, sent in lethal aid, and mobilized the Hezbollah. There must be consequences for these actions, and there are plenty of tools that we have at our disposal. I reject the utterly false narrative that Iran's and Russia's activities in Syria constitute counterterrorism.

I look forward to hearing from you, Mr. Blinken, on what actions the United States is considering, what are our options, and how can Congress be your partner.

Turning to Iraq just for a moment, if I might, the counter-ISIL fight is just the first step in restoring stability. I am cautiously optimistic that the military operation to push ISIL out of Mosul is resourced and planned to achieve its goals. And beyond the military operations, I want to raise the alarm bell about winning the peace. I think we will win the war, but can we win the peace? Iraqi leaders in Baghdad must get their act together. The past few months of political infighting and mud-throwing instilled no confidence that leaders in Baghdad, Irbil, and other provincial levels are prepared to put the Iraqi people first. We know that the Iraqi Security Forces, the Kurdish Peshmerga forces, and other forces cannot fight or bomb their way to a stable Iraq.

What will come after ISIL's defeat?

I am not confident that Iraqi leaders are sufficiently engaged to respond to the humanitarian crisis coming when hundreds of thousands of civilians flee Mosul. I am not confident that Iraqi leaders are effectively in control of the popular mobilization forces to prevent sectarian reprisal violence. I am not confident that Iraqi leaders are committed to recovering stabilization and governance plans that will give all Iraqis a stake in the peace.

Weeks ago, I would have said the situation in the region, particularly Syria, could not be any worse. Now we know that it can. Russia is guilty of war crimes for bombing a humanitarian aid convoy. Assad is barrel bombing Aleppo with impunity and using water access as a weapon, as if denying humanitarian aid was not sufficiently deplorable. These are crimes against humanity. The longer the Assad regime remains entrenched in Damascus and the longer ISIL and the Al Nusra Front remain active in the region, the more depraved the situation becomes, the more hopeless are innocent civilians, the more susceptible are vulnerable populations to violent extremism, and the more strained are governments in Jordan and Lebanon to respond to these pressures.

At risk is an entire generation of children in the region that have only known war and some governments that want to stand with them but have been unsuccessful. At risk is an entire generation of children who will only know refugee camps, who do not have access to clean water, health care, schools, and employment opportunities. This situation cannot continue. The U.S. must provide more decisive leadership to protect the civilian population.

Thank you, Mr. Chairman.

The CHAIRMAN. Mr. Ranking Member, I appreciate your comments. I think this is what we have been saying since about 2011.

My comments about Secretary Kerry being a sympathetic figure are really not negative towards him. He is out there without the ability to do diplomacy because everyone knows there is no backup plan in the event that diplomacy fails, which is a recipe for disaster. We have known that now for 5 years. So again, it was more of an indictment of the President than of our Secretary of State.

But with that, our Deputy Secretary of State, Tony Blinken, who we appreciate being here today as a substitute, we thank you for your service, and we look forward to your abbreviated comments. Your written testimony, without objection, will be entered into the record.

STATEMENT OF HON. ANTONY J. BLINKEN, DEPUTY SECRETARY OF STATE, U.S. DEPARTMENT OF STATE, WASHINGTON, D.C.

Mr. BLINKEN. Mr. Chairman, thank you very much. Let me just start by thanking you personally, as well as the committee staff, for your courtesy in rescheduling this hearing to today. As you noted, it was originally going to be yesterday. I very much appreciate it. It did allow me to make this trip to Turkey, which I am happy to talk about.

And Senator Cardin, thank you for referencing the best bilateral meeting I had during the week in New York at the U.N. General Assembly. My meeting with Grover was by far the most informative and interesting session.

Mr. Chairman, Ranking Member Cardin, members of the committee, thank you for this opportunity to discuss the civil war in Syria and its regional implications.

Now in its sixth year, the civil war has destroyed the fabric of life in Syria. It has killed at least 400,000 people, triggered the worst humanitarian displacement crisis since World War II, put neighboring countries of first asylum under enormous pressure, exacerbated regional tensions, helped swell the ranks of violent extremist organizations, most notably Daesh and Al Qaeda.

The conflict continues to be fueled by patrons and proxies with very divergent interests and priorities at a time of unprecedented upheaval in the wider Middle East, as governments pursue new models of political rule and vie for regional influence. In short, the Syria conflict presents one of the most complex challenges we have faced.

The United States is clear-eyed about our role and responsibility. The civil war in Syria is not about us, nor can it be solved solely by us. But it challenges our security and strategic interests and our moral values. So we are working to leverage our country's unique capacity to mobilize others to end the civil war and contend with its consequences, even as we lead the international coalition to counter and ultimately defeat Daesh. We are also working to facilitate aid to millions of Syrian civilians, both in Syria and outside of Syria, to try to reduce the human suffering the civil war has engendered.

Our primary task is to defeat Daesh, which poses the most immediate threat to our citizens, to our country, to our allies and partners. We have built an international coalition with 67 partners. We devised a comprehensive strategy to attack Daesh at its core in Iraq and Syria; dismantle its foreign fighter, financing, and recruitment networks; stop its external operations and confront its affiliates. We are aggressively implementing that strategy. And we are succeeding.

Our comprehensive campaign is systematically liberating territory from Daesh and denying its sanctuaries, cutting off its financing, stemming the flow of foreign fighters, combating its narrative, allowing citizens to return home, gutting the twisted foundation on which Daesh's global ambitions rest.

We have deprived Daesh of about 25 percent of the territory it once controlled in Syria and more than 50 percent of the territory it once controlled in Iraq.

And we now face a moment of both strategic opportunity and urgency.

The opportunity before us is to effectively eliminate Turkey's physical caliphate by taking back the last big pieces it holds: Mosul in Iraq and Raqqa and Dabiq in Syria. With support from the coalition, local forces are preparing to launch these operations in the period ahead. These battles will be hard, but the consequences to Daesh will be devastating, both practically and psychologically.

But this opportunity is matched by urgency. As the noose around Daesh is tightening, we have seen them try to adapt by plotting or encouraging indiscriminate attacks in as many places as possible. This puts a premium on destroying Daesh's external operations network, especially in Raqqa where many of these operations are plotted, planned, and directed.

In Iraq, Mr. Chairman, 2 weeks ago and then in Turkey this week, I held discussions with our partners on the campaign plan to liberate Mosul, Dabiq, and Raqqa. It requires extraordinary coordination not just militarily but also to ensure that we meet the humanitarian, stabilization, and governance needs of newly liberated territory. It will be this effort that ensures that Daesh, once defeated, stays defeated.

And, Senator Cardin, I think you are exactly right that in a sense the harder questions are almost what follows the military defeat of Daesh in Iraq and certainly in Syria. Ultimately we will not fully succeed in destroying Daesh until we resolve the civil war in Syria, which remains a powerful magnet for foreign terrorist organizations that thrive in war's ungoverned spaces and draw strength from Assad's destruction of his own nation.

The objectives and processes that we agreed to earlier this month with Russia were the right ones: a renewal of the cessation of hostilities, the immediate resumption of unhindered aid deliveries, the degradation of and focus on Daesh and Al Qaeda in Syria, the grounding of the Syrian air force over civilian populations, the beginning of a Syria-led negotiating track that can provide a pathway out of the conflict and make possible the restoration of a united, peaceful Syria.

The actions of the Assad regime and Russia, aided and abetted by jihadist spoilers, now risk fundamentally undermining this initiative, destroying what was the best prospect for ending the civil war. The September 19 attack on the U.N. humanitarian aid convoy in Big Orem near Aleppo was unconscionable. It has been followed by the regime and Russia renewing a horrific offensive in Aleppo that includes the killing of hundreds of innocent civilians and apparently intentional attacks on hospitals, the water supply network, other civilian infrastructure.

Yesterday, Mr. Chairman, Secretary Kerry informed the Foreign Minister of Russia that unless Russia takes immediate steps to end the assault on Aleppo and restore the cessation of hostilities, the United States will suspend U.S.-Russia bilateral engagement on Syria, including the establishment of the Joint Implementation Center. At President Obama's direction, we also are actively considering other options to advance our goal of ending the civil war and starting a political transition in Syria. We continue to maintain close links to the moderate opposition to support their viability.

It is important, as always, to remember how this crisis in Syria began, not with barrel bombs or chlorine, but with peaceful protests of citizens who were calling for peaceful change. The humanitarian catastrophe that we bear witness to is a direct outgrowth of Assad's vengeance against his own people, and indeed, the cost is rising every day for the region, for Europe, most of all for the Syrian people.

We will continue to work with the coalition we built to defeat Daesh, and we will explore and, as appropriate, pursue every option to end the civil war in Syria and bring about the political transition that the Syrian people want and deserve.

Thank you very much, Mr. Chairman.

[The prepared statement of Mr. Blinken follows:]

PREPARED STATEMENT OF ANTONY BLINKEN

INTRODUCTION

Chairman Corker, Ranking Member Cardin, members of the committee—thank you for the opportunity to come before you today to discuss the civil war in Syria and its regional implications.

Now in its sixth year, the crisis has destroyed the fabric of life in Syria, killed at least 400,000 people, triggered the worst human displacement crisis since the end of World War II, put neighboring countries of first asylum under enormous pressure, exacerbated regional tensions, and helped swell the ranks of violent extremist organizations, most notably Daesh and al-Qaeda.

The conflict continues to be fueled by patrons and proxies with divergent interests and priorities at a time of unprecedented upheaval across the wider Middle East, as governments pursue new models of political rule and vie for new positions of regional influence. In short, the Syrian conflict presents one of the most complex challenges we have faced.

There is no way to look at what is happening on the ground in Syria and not feel profound grief and horror. In the midst of such tragedy, it is tempting to want a neat answer that ends the civil war and eases suffering overnight. But the challenges before us defy silver bullet solutions.

The United States is clear-eyed about our role and responsibility. The civil war in Syria is not about us, nor can it be solved solely by us. But it challenges our security and strategic interests—and moral values. So we are leveraging our country's unique capacity to mobilize others to end the civil war and contend with its consequences, even as we lead the international coalition to counter and ultimately defeat Daesh. We are also harnessing the power of diplomacy to facilitate aid to millions of Syrian civilians and reduce human suffering in any way that we can.

DEFEATING DAESH

Our primary task is to defeat Daesh, which poses the most immediate threat to our citizens, our country, and our allies. We built an international coalition with 67 partners. We devised a comprehensive strategy to attack Daesh at its core in Iraq and Syria; dismantle its foreign fighter, financing and recruitment networks; stop its external operations and confront its affiliates. We are aggressively implementing that strategy. And we are succeeding.

Two years ago, Daesh was expanding its territory, building its status online as an irresistible magnet for budding violent extremists, and threatening to overrun even Baghdad and Erbil.

Today, momentum in the fight to defeat Daesh has shifted dramatically.

Our comprehensive campaign is systematically liberating territory from Daesh and denying its sanctuaries, cutting off its financing, stemming the flow of foreign fighters, combatting its narrative on social media, allowing citizens to return home, and gutting the twisted foundation on which Daesh's global ambitions rest.

Daesh has not had a major battlefield victory in well over a year. We've eliminated tens of thousands of fighters and more than one hundred mid-to-senior level leaders. We've destroyed thousands of pieces of equipment and weapons. We've deprived Daesh of about 25 percent of the territory it once controlled in Syria and more than 50 percent of the territory in Iraq.

Now, we face a moment of strategic opportunity and urgency.

The opportunity is to effectively eliminate Daesh's geographic caliphate by taking back the last big pieces it holds: Mosul in Iraq and Raqqa and Dabiq in Syria. With support from the coalition, local forces are preparing to launch these operations in the period ahead. It will not be easy. The enemy is dug in and desperate, but the consequences for Daesh will be devastating—practically and psychologically. It will lose critical havens from which to organize, plot and prosecute attacks. It will be deprived of critical resources that finance its activities. It will be denied key destinations for foreign fighter recruits. And it will lose the entire foundation of its narrative—the building of a physical caliphate.

This opportunity is matched by urgency. As the noose around Daesh closes, we've seen them try to adapt by plotting or encouraging indiscriminate attacks in as many places as possible: a market in Baghdad, a nightclub in Orlando, a promenade in Nice, a cafe in Dhaka, a bustling airport in Istanbul. Potential recruits are being told to stay home and attack there. Surviving foreign fighters are being pushed out of Iraq and Syria and back to where they came from. This puts a premium on destroying Daesh's external operations network—especially in Raqqa, where many of these operations are plotted, planned, and directed.

In Iraq two weeks ago and in Turkey this week, I held discussions with our partners on the campaign plan to liberate Mosul, Dabiq, and Raqqa. It requires extraordinary coordination not only militarily, but also to ensure that we meet the humanitarian, stabilization and governance needs of newly liberated territory.

Moreover, the fight to hold ground, rebuild cities, restore services, clear schools and clinics of IEDs, care for displaced children, help families return home, hold Daesh accountable, provide genuine security, re-establish the rule of law—in other words, the fight to provide for the basic needs of a nation and prevent the emergence of Daesh 2.0 is only just beginning. The way we're doing this—working not only with a broad international coalition but also with local partners on the ground who know the territory and have a stake in stabilizing and governing it—helps ensure that Daesh's defeat will be sustainable and lasting.

As Iraqi forces and humanitarian workers prepare for the liberation of Mosul, this task must be matched by steps towards inclusive political and economic progress. We strongly support Prime Minister Abadi's leadership on reform and reconciliation. He has begun critical outreach to Sunnis, announced "zero tolerance" for human rights abuses, and reached an agreement with the Kurds to restart oil exports from Kirkuk.

All Iraqis—be they Sunni, Shia, Christian, Arab, or Kurd, or any other—have to be convinced that the state that they've been asked to fight for will stand up for their rights and their equities, that they can advance their interests more effectively as citizens of a united Iraq than as supplicants of other regional powers or members of isolated competitive blocs in a fractured and weakened state. It will be this effort that ensures that Daesh once defeated stays defeated.

RESPONDING TO SYRIAN CIVIL WAR

Ultimately, we will not succeed in fully destroying Daesh until we resolve the civil war in Syria, which remains a powerful magnet for foreign terrorist organizations that thrive in the war's ungoverned spaces and draw strength from Assad's brutal destruction of his own nation.

We know from history and experience that civil wars end in one of three ways. First, one side wins. That is unlikely in Syria because as soon as one side gets the advantage, the outside patrons of the other side intensify their engagement to right the balance.

Second, the parties exhaust themselves. Typically, that takes a decade—or longer when a multiplicity of actors are involved. The civil war in Syria is entering year six, and it features a broad array of internal and external actors with different priorities.

Third and finally, civil wars end when external powers intervene either militarily or politically. But military intervention typically adds fuel to the fire, extending before ending the conflict and suffering. In the case of Syria, short of a wholesale invasion that no outside power has the interest to undertake, military intervention is not likely to be decisive. That leaves a political intervention, with key outside powers and patrons shaping, supporting and imposing a resolution. That is the effort we have been engaged in with Russia and other members of the International Syria Support Group, building on the foundation of the Geneva communiques and U.N. Security Council resolutions.

The objectives and the processes we agreed to earlier this month were and are the right ones: a renewal of the cessation of hostilities, the immediate resumption of unhindered aid deliveries, the degradation of and focus on Daesh and Al-Qaeda in Syria, which is also known as Nusra, the grounding of the Syrian air force over civilian populations and the beginning of a Syrian-led negotiating track that can provide a pathway out of the conflict and make possible the restoration of a united and peaceful Syria. The United States, as Secretary Kerry has said, will make absolutely no apology for going the extra mile to try to stop the violence and ease the suffering of the Syrian people. It would be diplomatic malpractice to close the door on our larger goal of keeping alive the prospect of a political accommodation.

Tragically, the actions of the Assad regime and Russia, aided and abetted by jihadist spoilers, now risk fatally undermining this initiative—destroying the best prospect for ending the civil war. The September 19 attack on a U.N. humanitarian aid convoy in Big Orem near Aleppo was unconscionable. It has been followed by the regime and Russia renewing a horrific offensive in Aleppo that includes the killing of hundreds of innocent civilians and apparently intentional attacks on hospitals, the water supply network, and other civilian infrastructure.

Yesterday, Secretary Kerry informed the Foreign Minister of Russia that unless Russia takes immediate steps to end the assault on Aleppo and restore the cessation of hostilities, the United States will suspend U.S.-Russia bilateral engagement on Syria—including the establishment of the Joint Implementation Center. At President Obama's direction, we also are actively considering other options to advance our goal of ending the civil war and starting a political transition in Syria. We continue to maintain close links to the moderate opposition to support their viability.

RESPONDING TO HUMANITARIAN DISASTER

The humanitarian catastrophe is a direct outgrowth of Assad's vengeance against his own people, and the human and financial cost of the conflict rises every day—for the region, for Europe, but most of all, for Syrians.

Eighty-one percent of Syria's population requires humanitarian assistance—6.5 million Syrians are displaced in their own country. And 4.8 million Syrians have fled to neighboring countries—straining the capacity of generous host communities in Turkey, Lebanon, Jordan, Iraq, and Egypt.

Across the region, more than three million children are out of school, and many of their parents do not have access to legal employment. As a result, refugees are putting themselves at risk and traveling farther and farther afield in pursuit of a hope shared by parents the world over: a better future for their children.

The United States—as the world's leading humanitarian donor—has worked with heroic partners on the ground, including U.N. agencies and NGOs, to help strengthen the resilience of refugees as well as the communities that host them.

Since the start of the crisis, we have provided over $5.9 billion in humanitarian aid to the response inside Syria and across the region, in addition to development assistance to Jordan and Lebanon, and we have worked with the World Bank to develop new types of affordable loans for middle-income countries grappling with protracted crises. We have provided nearly $1.1 billion in humanitarian assistance to Iraq since 2014—including a recent tranche of funding to preposition food supplies and basic relief items ahead of Mosul's liberation.

Last week, President Obama convened 52 countries and international organizations for a summit during the U.N. General Assembly, where the nations made measurable commitments to increase humanitarian contributions by $4.5 billion; double the number of refugees who are offered resettlement or other legal forms of admissions; and increase the number of refugee children in school globally and refugee adults working by one million each.

Galvanizing these resources is vital to helping shore up an international response system that, for all its extraordinary efforts, is overstretched, overburdened, and overwhelmed.

CONCLUSION

It is important, as always, to remember how the crisis in Syria began—not with barrel bombs and chlorine, but with peaceful protests of citizens calling for change.

When nations squeeze out moderate voices, they create a vacuum filled by extremists. When people feel shut out, their sense of alienation and marginalization sharpens divisions that extremists love to exploit.

That is why the United States is working for a settlement in Syria that will give people viable choices other than supporting Assad for fear of terrorists or terrorists for fear of Assad.

That is why we support a peace process for Yemen that reunites the country rather than deepening sectarian divisions that have already left the nation vulnerable to exploitation by Al Qaeda in the Arabian Peninsula and Daesh.

It is why we are supporting Prime Minister al-Sarraj's efforts to achieve national reconciliation and build a unity government that represents all Libyan people and unites them against Daesh. Under Prime Minister al-Sarraj's leadership, Libyan ground forces have made significant progress against Daesh in recent months. The United States responded to the Prime Minister's request for help in this effort, conducting over 170 counter-Daesh airstrikes under Operation Odyssey Lightning. Daesh now holds less than one square kilometer of Sirte's city center.

It is why we have urged greater space for peaceful dissent in Egypt, as we offer assistance to increase Egypt's capabilities to counter a Daesh-affiliated insurgency in Sinai.

It can be hard to look back on the events in this region in the last few years and feel a great deal of optimism. But we must persist, and we intend to work with the coalition we've built to defeat Daesh, end the civil war in Syria, and bring about the political transition that the Syrian people want.

The CHAIRMAN. Thank you, Mr. Secretary.

I am just going to ask one question and then may interject as we go along.

From your perspective, having been both at the White House and now the State Department in important roles, is it your observation that the only way for our foreign policy endeavors and for the Secretary of State to be successful is for there to be a close relationship between the White House and the Secretary of State and that the Secretary have the knowledge that the White House will back up the initiatives that he or she endeavors to achieve?

Mr. BLINKEN. I think, Mr. Chairman, in any administration you certainly want——

The CHAIRMAN. That is a yes.

Mr. BLINKEN [continuing]. A close relationship among——

The CHAIRMAN. We have had, I know, a number of proposals from the State Department, including the no-fly zone in the northwest triangle of Aleppo and the air exclusion zone along the Turkish-Syrian border that the Turks supported. Why is it that in that case, in the case right now where Secretary Kerry is out there on a tether—you just mentioned that we are going to cut off bilateral negotiations on Syria. I just have a feeling that is just not much of a price to pay from Russia's standpoint.

So there have been discussions of Plan B. Secretary Kerry talked to several of us in Munich in February about the cessation discussions, and there was going to be a Plan B if they failed. I have never seen signs of a Plan B. I know Russia does not believe there is a Plan B. Assad does not believe there is a Plan B. Iran does not believe there is a Plan B. So when I say that and refer to Secretary Kerry as a sympathetic figure, I say that because how can a Secretary of State have any chance of success in ending the murder, the torture, the rape, the bombing of innocent people, the killing of young people when the White House is unwilling at any level to have a backup if diplomacy fails?

Mr. BLINKEN. Mr. Chairman, on all of these issues, including Syria, we work through a very deliberative process involving all of the agencies relevant to the issue at the NSC, with the State Department, with the Pentagon, with the intelligence agencies, et cetera. And we try to work through these things deliberately and make the best possible assessment of the best way to advance our objectives and our interests and to evaluate both the benefits and risks of any course of action. And that is what we have done in this case. And the policy that emerges is the product of these deliberations that the Secretary of State is very much fully a part of.

In the case of Syria, it is useful to step back and ask ourselves this question: How do civil wars typically end? And we know from history and experience that they end in one of two ways.

The CHAIRMAN. I do not want a history lesson. I would like to understand what Plan B is, the mysterious Plan B that has been referred to since February, the mysterious Plan B that was supposed to be leverage to get Russia to quit killing innocent people, to get Assad to quit killing innocent people. Just explain to us the elements of Plan B.

Mr. BLINKEN. Two things, Mr. Chairman.

In the first instance, Plan B is the consequence of the failure, as a result of Russia's actions, of Plan A in that what is likely to happen now, if the agreement cannot be followed through on and Russia reneges totally on its commitments——

The CHAIRMAN. Which it has.

Mr. BLINKEN [continuing]. Which it appears to have done. This is going, of course, to be bad for everyone, but it is going to be bad first and foremost——

The CHAIRMAN. I want to hear about Plan B. I understand all the context here.

Mr. BLINKEN. I think, sir, this is important because Russia has a profound incentive in trying to make this work. It cannot win in Syria. It can only prevent Assad from losing. If this now gets to the point where the civil war actually accelerates, all of the outside patrons are going to throw in more and more weaponry against Russia. Russia will be left propping up Assad in an ever-smaller piece of Syria.

The CHAIRMAN. All of us understand that. What is Plan B? Give me the elements of Plan B.

Mr. BLINKEN. So two things. Again, the consequences I think to Russia, as well as to the regime, will begin to be felt as a result of Plan A not being implemented because of Russia's actions.

Second, as I indicated, the President has asked all of the agencies to put forward options, some familiar, some new that we are very actively reviewing. When we are able to work through these in the days ahead, we will have an opportunity to come back and talk about them in detail. But we are in the process of doing that.

The CHAIRMAN. Okay. So let me just say what we already know. There is no Plan B. When I referred to Secretary Kerry as a sympathetic figure, I said that because he gets up every day, without any support. Some say he should resign over lack of support or at least threaten to. It is impossible to be successful in negotiating an agreement with someone if there are no consequences. In this case, the consequences that you are laying out is that Russia will fully determine the future of Syria.

Mr. BLINKEN. I think Russia is going to bear very significant consequences over the failure of this——

The CHAIRMAN. So far, that has not been the case, and I know that is what the President said when they came in and stepped into the vacuum a year ago.

So, I rest my case. Diplomacy without any plan of failure is something that cannot be successful. Again, based on my experiences this weekend with an administration that is unwilling to even sit down and talk about a solution with the people who are involved because they think this is bad for our country, but unwilling to sit down and talk about a possible option just leads me to believe that we will continue to have non-success in Syria, non-success in other areas.

Again, all of us have tremendous sadness over the fact that our country has idly sat by after encouraging the people of Syria. If you remember, Ambassador Ford was cheering these people on—cheering these people on. We made commitments to the opposition, which General Idris—I remember meeting with him in Turkey. We could not even get him the trucks that we committed.

So it is a statement without a plan. It is the statement of redlines without follow-up. Again, I fear that more bad results are going to occur.

With that, I will turn it to Senator Menendez.

Senator MENENDEZ. Well, thank you, Mr. Chairman.

And let me thank the ranking member for yielding time. We have had a train derailment in New Jersey with fatalities, so I need to get back. So I appreciate the opportunity. This is an incredibly important topic.

So I think we had a lot of missed opportunities when this committee passed not unanimously but a strong bipartisan vote to train and to assist the vetted Syrian rebels, moderate Syrian rebels at the time that that could be done and gave the President the power and the wherewithal to do that. It was not done then.

Then when it was done, it was done so feebly that those who we trained were largely eliminated.

And then instead of having a safe zone, which many of us called for, which would have given individuals the opportunity to have an ability for security and maybe to organize those who might want to fight for their country, that was not done.

And so I move forward and I see what has happened to date. Of course, your written testimony is much longer, but there is one paragraph of it that I think is incredibly important to talk about. You talked about Daesh, but you say in your statement on page 3: "Ultimately we will not succeed in fully destroying Daesh until we resolve the civil war in Syria, which remains a powerful magnet for foreign terrorist organizations that thrive in the war's ungoverned spaces and draw strength from Assad's brutal destruction of his own nation." And I fully agree. That is the problem here, having missed opportunities and now creating a vacuum where Russia comes in.

I know that I keep hearing the equation that Russia will ultimately come to an understanding that it is paying very large consequences for its participation. That has not changed their calculations at all. As a matter of fact, they avoid Assad in this process. I think that the temporary truce that was created, from the Russian perspectives, never had a real calculation to actually effectuate the results of what Secretary Kerry intended, which of course I would have applauded. But it was to give Assad the ability to rearm and reorganize, and then immediately the incredible, despicable attacks made against humanitarian convoys.

So my question is this. I would have asked what Plan B is, too. I do not get a sense that there is one, and that worries me. I do not think we should wait for the next President to start devising something that moves in that direction. And I understand that Secretary Kerry has threatened to end bilateral talks with Russia over Syria.

But I cannot fathom, for the life of me, what those talks are producing anyhow. I mean, Russia seems to agree only for the purposes of giving Assad time to rearm and regroup. What leverage do we really have? What are we doing here to Russia to change its calculation? Because now, whether we like it or not, they are the major player here. And I have had a totally different view that Russia does not share our end goals here. It does not have the same interests as we do. It has a very different set of interests.

So understanding that, give me a sense specifically of what leverage do we have. Why are we still engaged in a conversation in which we have a, quote/unquote, partner that continues to undermine our purposes in Syria, as well as that of the international community, which is why I understand some British and French counterparts walked out of a meeting recently at the U.N.

Mr. BLINKEN. Thank you, Senator.

Two things.

First, we believe that the effort that we have made to reach this agreement with Russia was the best way to effectively move toward ending the civil war because had it succeeded—and, indeed, it still can succeed and I think we will know in the hours ahead whether Russia is responsive or not—the cessation of hostilities would be restored, humanitarian assistance would flow. You would get the Syrian air force out of the skies over civilian populated areas. Russia would be focused, as it claims it has been on Daesh.

Senator MENENDEZ. So we understand the benefit if it had succeeded. Let us presume for argument's sake that it is not going to succeed because Russia does not want it to.

Mr. BLINKEN. So, again, I know that this may not fully resonate, but, first, Russia escalated its engagement in Syria because it has been there all along. It has been there for years—precisely because it was at risk of losing its only foothold in the Middle East. And it came in harder in order to save Assad from falling at a time when it looked like he would, although I think that assessment was probably overly optimistic. It is now in a position where, having gotten in, it is very, very hard to get out because Assad cannot win. They can prevent him from losing, but he cannot win. So they are stuck.

In the first instance, the leverage is again the consequences for Russia of being stuck in a quagmire that is going to have a number of profoundly negative effects.

First, they are going to be bearing the brunt, if the civil war escalates as a result of their actions, of an onslaught of weaponry coming in from outside patrons.

Second, they will be seen in their own country and throughout the world and in the region as complicit with Assad, with Hezbollah, and with Iran in the slaughter of Sunni Muslims—5 percent of their own population is Muslim.

Senator MENENDEZ. But do we agree they are already complicit on that?

Mr. BLINKEN. Indeed, but this is only going to get worse if the civil war gets worse as a result of their actions.

Any efforts that they have been making to peel away countries, for example, on Ukraine I think the international disgust at the actions that they are taking in Aleppo will make that even more difficult than it already is. So all of these consequences are there.

But as I said in response also to the chairman's question, we are also very actively looking at additional options that we can bring to bear to advance our objectives in Syria. And those objectives are ending the civil war and getting a political transition.

Senator MENENDEZ. I know what the objectives are. I just do not see that the consequences that you are suggesting can be leveraged.

Thank you, Mr. Chairman.

The CHAIRMAN. Thank you.

I know Senator Rubio is here, but he wants to get adapted. If you could go ahead, that would be great.

Senator CARDIN. Thank you, Mr. Chairman.

Thank you, Secretary Blinken, again.

What has happened has happened, and I think history will reflect decisions that were made and whether they were the right decisions at the time. We need to learn from the past and decide how to move forward.

There is no question that there is an urgent need to protect human life, civilian life, in Syria, and the United States needs to act boldly.

I am encouraged, Secretary Blinken, by your comments that there will be very significant consequences for Russia's actions. I look forward to seeing how that is translated into U.S. policy and U.S. international leadership, working with other countries. We need bold U.S.-led actions to protect civilian lives. We need that now, and I look forward to reviewing with you the options that are being considered and the actions that are taken to protect civilian life and the significant consequences concerning Russia.

I want to ask you a specific question. Could Russia have stopped the Assad regime from what it has done in the last several weeks? And does Russia have enough influence over the Assad regime to change their behavior?

Mr. BLINKEN. I believe the answer is yes.

Senator CARDIN. Number two, Iran has been extremely engaged in Syria. I have not seen the U.S. take action or work with the international community to take action against Iran in regards to their support of terrorism in Syria. Are we restricted because of the JCPOA? My understanding is that the terms of the JCPOA do not restrict us, but have there been diplomatic restrictions as a result of the JCPOA that has limited our ability to hold Iran responsible for its actions in Syria?

Mr. BLINKEN. The answer is no, Senator.

Senator CARDIN. So why have we not taken action against Iran?

Mr. BLINKEN. We have, and indeed we continue with regard to Iran——

Senator CARDIN. With regard to their activities in Syria?

Mr. BLINKEN. Yes, sanctioned activities, entities that have——

Senator CARDIN. New sanctions have been imposed?

Mr. BLINKEN. Sanctions have been imposed on entities in Iran that have sought to do business or support the regime.

Senator CARDIN. I understand we have sanctions that are related to their nefarious actions other than the nuclear activities, but I am not aware that we have increased those sanctions or have looked at ways in which we can apply more pressure against Iran. It is my understanding we have been pretty guarded in these activities.

Mr. BLINKEN. We put in place at the very outset of the crisis, you know, various sanctions with regard to Syria to isolate and put pressure on the regime, and those sanctions also include sanctioning individuals or entities who do business in various ways with the regime, with the military, et cetera. And in that context, my understanding is that Iranian entities and individuals have been sanctioned.

Senator CARDIN. You had said that we are looking—the President instructed to look at all options in regards to the current crisis in Syria. Is part of that taking action against Iran?

Mr. BLINKEN. I do not want to get ahead of where we are in our discussions. But Iran is clearly, along with its proxy, Hezbollah, the most serious impediment to ending the civil war in that its support for the regime is the most significant of all. Now, as I said at the outset, I believe that given the support that Russia has provided, support that has gotten greater since Russia increased its engagement in Syria, it too has the capacity to change the actions of the regime. But there is no question that Iran and Hezbollah are arguably the most important outside supporters of the regime.

Senator CARDIN. Well, I think you would agree with me that since the JCPOA has been agreed upon, Iran has shown no slowing down of their activities in Syria. So I would hope that we would see some aggressive U.S. leadership to make it clear that that conduct does not get a free pass because of the JCPOA. So I would hope that that would be part of the options that are being considered.

And let me also say in regards to Russia, it is not an isolated problem we are having with Russia. Russia has attacked America through cyber, trying to compromise our electoral process. Russia has violated the Minsk agreements and is causing Ukraine to be compromised today. And I could list a lot of other activities that Russia is participating in.

So as we look at very significant consequences that Russia will face as a result of their failure to live up to the ceasefire agreements, I hope that in that equation will go these other activities so that there is a very clear message to Russia that U.S. leadership will not tolerate that type of conduct, and we are prepared to take unilateral action. We are also prepared to work with the willing to make sure there is a price to be paid for their activities.

Thank you, Mr. Chairman.

The CHAIRMAN. Thank you, Mr. Ranking Member. I am sure that there will be more said. I would love at some time, if there is a Plan B, to have a classified briefing if that is what it takes. I think we all understand that it is nonexistent, and the only thing that is existent is words.

Senator Rubio?

Senator RUBIO. Thank you.

Thank you, Secretary Blinken, for being here.

In your statement, you mention Russia six times, as you should. They are clearly involved, but there is an omission. I do not believe that in your testimony you mention Iran a single time. And in fact, until Senator Cardin just raised it, I am not sure it had been discussed yet in terms of Iran's role in this region.

Earlier this month, you said you could not guarantee to the American people that the funds that Iran has received, as a result of the payments that were made and of the JCPOA, have not been used for terrorism. I think it is common sense that in fact they would do that. We have seen, for example, press reports that Iran's Guardian Counsel instructed its central bank to transfer $1.7 billion to the military of Iran. And by the way, I do not think that number is a coincidence. So we have see the top IRGC commander last week say that the IRGC and its allies supply intelligence for Russian airstrikes in Syria.

And so I think the first thing we have to point to here is the fact that these pallets of taxpayer dollars that have been allowed to Iran have ultimately helped them help Russia target innocent Syrians in this quest to increase their dominance in the region or their role in the region and to prop up Assad.

Again, I do not know how we justify the transfer of all of these funds to the Iranian regime knowing that the Iranian regime is deeply involved in propping up the Assad regime and in the process providing assistance to all these atrocities that are now being committed by both Assad and the Russians. How do we justify that?

Mr. BLINKEN. Thank you, Senator.

First, as you know, because you have been so focused on this for many years, Iran has been engaged in the support of terrorism and destabilizing activities, including in Syria, for a long time during sanctions, in other words, before the nuclear agreement, during the negotiation of the agreement, and indeed, since sanctions have been lifted in the context of that agreement. So their conduct has been consistent throughout. And, again, they were doing this before when we had the sanctions regime in place because of their nuclear program.

The one thing that has changed is we have taken a nuclear weapon off the table far into the future, which is profoundly good for our interests and the interests of our partners and allies.

But as we have said all along, we fully expected that they would continue to take these actions in various ways in various places after the agreement. That is why we have worked very hard to continue and, indeed, to increase our efforts to counter them.

So we have worked very closely, as you know, with the Gulf partners building up their capacity. We just signed a record-breaking MOU with Israel to make sure that they have in place over the next decade what they need for their security, and we continue to implement sanctions against Iranian entities.

Senator RUBIO. So the one thing has changed that basically they were involved in terror before, they are involved in terror now—and I consider their support of Assad to be part of that—that the only thing that has changed is that now we have made it harder for them to acquire a nuclear weapons capability.

I would say a second thing has changed. They now have access to millions and millions of dollars they did not have access to before. So you have the world's key sponsor of terrorism now has millions of dollars more than they once did. There is no evidence that they are using it to build hospitals, bridges, roads, orphanages, sponsor food programs around the world. We do not see aid convoys from Iran providing food and medicine to people suffering in Syria.

What we see is an increased amount of support for the Assad regime and the sponsorship of terrorism.

So one of the things that has changed is they now have access to millions of dollars they did not have a year and a half ago.

Mr. BLINKEN. Senator, our best assessment——

Senator RUBIO. Billions. I apologize. Billions.

Mr. BLINKEN. Our best assessment is that given Iran's very significant economic difficulties, the vast bulk of the resources that they have had access to as a result of the agreement or as a result of The Hague settlement—these funds have been dedicated to the domestic economy, not to regional activities. Under the nuclear agreement, we believe that they now have access to roughly $50 billion that had been frozen or restricted in foreign accounts. They need half a trillion dollars to meet their investment needs, government obligations, propping up their currency, et cetera. And as I said, they have engaged, alas, in these activities before, during, and after. And also, unfortunately, a lot of support that they are providing to terror to proxies is not very resource-intensive. So that is why even as we have implemented the agreement, which in our judgment is a very good thing for our security and that of our allies and partners, we have worked to intensify our efforts to counter these activities.

Senator RUBIO. But even if we assume what you said is true, that the money has been used to prop up their domestic economy, ultimately if that were the case, that domestic economy would then produce more revenue that they could use to fulfill the funding needs of their priorities, which is terrorism and the propping up of Assad.

I guess the point for the average American who is watching this issue here is the bottom line. You have the world's supreme sponsor of terrorism who now has billions of dollars more than they once did as a result of this, and we are somehow supposed to believe that the bulk of it is being spent to improve the way their economy functions and that somehow, because funds are fungible, that this is not being used to increase their other aims that they have around the world and that includes the propping up of this extraordinarily vicious regime of Assad and their enablers in Russia.

So, again, I think this is just another example of how this deal and everything that surrounds it has now provided more resources to the Iranian regime to continue to do what they did. And one of the things they do with the money that they have been given is they are able to fund their intelligence gathering capabilities that allow them to help the Russians with their airstrikes, and those are the airstrikes that struck a convoy a week ago. Those are the airstrikes that are decimating Aleppo and creating a situation on the ground that we have not seen in decades anywhere in the world.

The CHAIRMAN. Thank you.

Senator Shaheen?

Senator SHAHEEN. Secretary Blinken, thank you for being here this morning.

Sadly, I have to say that I share my colleague's views that despite the best intentions that our policies in Syria have contributed to where we are today. There was a news report that just came over that Russia has rejected our demands for a resumption of a Syrian ceasefire and that they vowed today to press ahead with their operations in Syria. So I guess that says to me—and I think the news has been very clear—that Russia has escalated the civil war in Syria and they intend to continue to do that and Assad intends to continue to do that no matter what the expense is to his own people.

So I am not going to beat the Plan B horse because I appreciate that you have not been able to share with us what might be being considered. And maybe you are not able to talk about what options are being discussed that we might still have in Syria. But it seems to me that we need to look at all of those options because the current effort is not working. And I appreciate the arguments you are making. I just do not think they are working.

So let me go on to a couple of other areas where I am interested in what you can share with us.

On the Leaders' Summit on Refugees, I thought your appearing on Sesame Street was a good thing. It is nice to let young people know what is going on.

But can you talk about which states have been particularly generous, what has come out of that summit, what is being looked at to implement the commitments that have been made at the refugee summit?

Mr. BLINKEN. Thank you very much, Senator.

As you know and as the committee knows, we are facing the largest single wave of human displacement since World War II. Syria, of course, is what is generating a lot of it, but it is actually a global problem, a global crisis because we see forced migration of one kind or another virtually on every continent. In Africa alone, there are about 12 countries where people are, in effect, forcibly displaced by conflict. Central America, Afghanistan, Pakistan, around the world.

So the President brought together countries and leaders from around the world at this summit in New York on the margins of the General Assembly to take action, not just to talk about the problem, but to do something about it. And that is exactly what we did and what he did.

There were three objectives that we had going into the summit.

One was to get more resources from around the world into the humanitarian support system because, as the committee knows, unfortunately, it is significantly underfunded and it is basically overmatched by the scale and scope of the problems that we are facing. So we wanted to get more resources in, and we wanted to get countries that had not participated as much to participate or to do more. And we succeeded. We have got countries, all told, to put in for this next year, about 30 percent more than they did in 2015. So we are looking at billions of additional dollars for the humanitarian system.

Second, we were looking for countries to make additional commitments to resettle refugees, and we sought to basically double the number of legally resettled persons around the world over the next year. That objective, based on the commitments that were made, was also achieved.

Third and finally, we wanted to help build the resilience of countries that are receiving refugees, basically the country of first refuge and asylum, in the case of Syria, Turkey, Lebanon, and Jordan, which as the committee knows, have borne extraordinary burdens with millions of refugees. We wanted to increase support to them, but we also wanted them to make additional commitments to make sure that children could go to school and adults could go to work because, as Senator Cardin said, we do risk a lost generation of children from these conflicts if they are not able to go to school. We now have commitments over the next year for there to be an additional 1 million places in schools around the world for refugee children and another 1 million jobs, legal jobs, around the world. So these are significant. These are real. These are concrete.

That said, ultimately, the answer to a lot of this has to be resolving the underlying conflicts that are causing people to flee, to leave their homes, to leave their families in some cases, to put their lives and their children in jeopardy. We recognize that, and that, of course, is why it is so important to work to end this conflict in Syria.

But we did make a major advance. Now the critical thing will be to make sure the countries make good on their commitments, and we will be looking at that very carefully.

Senator SHAHEEN. Thank you. My time is up. So I will wait for the next round for other questions.

The CHAIRMAN. Thank you.

Senator Murphy?

Senator MURPHY. Thank you very much, Mr. Chairman.

Thank you, Mr. Secretary, for being with us today.

A comment and then a question.

So at the heart of the most spectacular U.S. foreign policy failures of the last 50 years is hubris, is this idea that there is a U.S. solution, usually a U.S. military solution, to every problem in the world. You can read Vietnam and Iraq and Libya through that lens. And this idea that is sort of being proffered on this committee, frankly by both sides of the aisle, but there are these clear alternatives to the current policy in Syria or Iraq that would lead to a radically different reality on the ground is fantasy. I hate the place that we are in today. It is an ongoing global tragedy.

But this idea that there was a magical moment in 2012 where we could have parachuted arms to the Syrian rebels and they would have overrun Assad is not true. Russia and Iran have had for a very long time equities in that country that are unequal to ours. They were always going to come to the defense of Assad with ferocity.

This idea that a safe zone would magically change the reality on the ground is a fantasy as well. Our own military leaders have thrown cold water on this idea because it would involve some major ground forces to make it meaningful, and there are very few people in this Congress who are willing to support the major deployment of U.S. ground forces.

I just say this because maybe, just maybe every bad thing that happens in the world is not a fault of failed U.S. policy. And maybe, just maybe there are times and there are places where there is not always a U.S. answer. Now, I think we can be incredibly helpful. I think that we can work with partners to try to make this situation better.

But I read the last 3 years as a continued ramp-up, albeit it very slowly, of U.S. military engagement in Syria and the situation on the ground for the Syrian people getting worse and worse and worse, not better and better and better. And I think history should probably teach us that those two things are likely not a coincidence.

I reject the idea that there are easy, clear alternatives that the administration just is not looking at. This is a hard problem with no easy solutions, and we should operate from an assumption that there are not always U.S.-led solutions to terrible, intractable problems in the world.

Let me ask you a question about where this failing of hubris could get us in trouble in the coming weeks and months, and that is in Mosul. So a new announcement that we are going to put 600 more U.S. military personnel on the ground to help retake Mosul, not an announcement that we are going to make a diplomatic surge in and around Mosul to try to solve some of the governance problems in that city. So share with us, maybe share with me in answer to my skepticism that a military surge in Mosul is ultimately going to solve the political problems that you correctly identify as the most intractable. We do not have a military quagmire in Iraq. We could solve the military problem in a heartbeat by putting another 200,000 U.S. troops back in. We have a political problem.

And so Mosul seems to me to be an example of where you have responded to pressure to try to make progress by announcing a military surge. I have no doubt that with 600 or 1,200 or 1,400 U.S. troops we will get the military objective that we want in Mosul. But how does that get us the political solution? Nineveh is an incredibly diverse province and what allowed for ISIS to overrun Mosul in the first place was not a military vacuum. It was a political vacuum in that city. So how do we make sure that there is a political component here so that our military hubris that we often have does not get us in the same, exact situation that it has over and over again in that region?

Mr. BLINKEN. Senator, if I have a chance, I would like to come back to your opening comment, but I want to answer your question.

Mosul is and will be the culmination in the Iraq side of the theater of the counter-ISIL or counter-Daesh campaign. And as I said at the outset in my opening remarks, it is a vitally important opportunity to deny ISIL its physical or geographic caliphate, which has been at the heart of its narrative and at the heart of its ability to project success. So it is vitally important.

But your comments are also vitally important because you are exactly right, that this cannot be and, indeed, is not just a military effort. We are working along multiple tracks at the same time in a coordinated fashion. On the military piece, making sure that all of the forces are coordinated under one plan with Iraqi leadership, but bringing in all of the critical elements to include the Iraqi Security Forces, the Kurdish Peshmerga, and critically tribal elements from Nineveh. There is now an objective of raising about 15,000 members from the tribes, and we are well on track to do that. That is part one.

Part two is making sure that we have in place all of the capacity we need to deal with what are likely to be the humanitarian consequences of seizing Mosul and, in particular, internally displaced persons. The U.N. is projecting that there could be up to a million people forced to flee Mosul as a result of the effort to liberate it. We are working very hard with the U.N., with the Iraqis to put in place everything that they need to care for these people with food, with shelter, with medicine. And that also is on track. It is challenging, but it is on track. We have raised the money to do it. We are prepositioning resources.

Third, stabilization of Mosul itself after it is liberated so that people have something to go back to as quickly as possible. There too we have raised significant resources. We have a plan in place to do that, to restore basic services, basic security.

Fourth and finally, you are exactly right. Governance—because unless the basic governance structure is in place and everyone agrees to it, we are going to have problems after the liberation. We have worked very hard with the Iraqi Government, with the Kurds, with other actors to make sure there is basic agreement on what governance will look like in Mosul and in Nineveh more generally, centered on the governor, who is the constitutionally appropriate person for the province, the provincial council, but also persons designated by Baghdad and by Irbil to support them and the city itself, in effect, divided up into eight quadrants with sub-mayors to make sure that, as much as possible, those making decisions are very closely representative of the people for whom they are making decisions.

So this is a coordinated effort. And you are exactly right. It has to bring in all of these elements, and that is exactly what we are working on.

We have also tried to learn lessons from the past. In Fallujah, when it was liberated, as you know, we saw some reprisal atrocities committed by the Shia PMF, popular mobilization forces. We have made sure that for Mosul there will be no southern or Shia PMF going into Mosul City, similarly no Kurdish Peshmerga going in, and as I said, a significant hold force comprised of members of Sunni tribes from the region, both in the security forces and in the police. So we have tried to learn from that. And also, as IDPs leave Mosul and are screened before they go to find refuge provided to them by the government and by the United Nations, we want to make sure that that process is done as quickly as possible, keeping families together, and again without any of the divisive elements being part of it, including the Shia PMF. So we very much have that in mind.

Just very quickly on your initial comment. I do think it is very important that we not be bound by history but we be informed by it. And in the case of Syria, we do know this. Civil wars throughout history have ended basically in one of three ways.

One side wins. That is not likely to happen anytime soon in Syria because the dynamic that we have seen is that as soon as one side gets the advantage, the outside patrons of the other side come in with more and right the balance. And that has been what has happened. So what the dynamic is outside patrons can make sure that no one loses in Syria, but it is very, very hard to make sure that one side wins.

The second way these things end is the parties exhaust themselves. Tragically what we see in history at least is that that takes on average 10 years. Syria is in year 6. And when there are a multiplicity of actors involved, it takes even longer.

The third way these things end is some kind of outside intervention, either military or political. Military intervention of the scale necessary to actually end the conflict is technically possible, but then whoever does that is going to be left holding a very, very heavy bag with all of the unintended consequences that will flow from that. And I do not think the United States nor, for that matter, Russia or any other actor is prepared to do that. That leaves, in effect, outside powers, the United Nations and others trying to put in place and, as necessary, impose some kind of political resolution. That is what we have been working on because we have seen that as the best way to try to end this.

The CHAIRMAN. Thank you.

I always appreciate my friend, Senator Murphy's comments and perspective,. and I think hubris certainly is something that can be the downfall of us all.

I will say that hubris also, from the standpoint of making big statements about what the United States is going to do, raises people's expectations. I think we certainly have made bold statements about what we were going to do relative to Syria that were followed up with almost nothing. And in that case, we have caused the sons and daughters and brothers and uncles and sisters of those in the Syrian opposition to be slaughtered as they waited for those things that we stated we were going to do but never did.

Senator Markey?

Senator MARKEY. Thank you, Mr. Chairman, very much.

Secretary Blinken, last October, former President Jimmy Carter wrote in the *New York Times* that since 2011, the United States' precondition that, quote, Assad must go, has reinforced escalation of Syria's civil war and inhibited serious discussion about compromise solutions.

Last Wednesday, President Carter published a follow-up piece in the *Times* calling on the entire international community to focus for now on just one imperative: stop the killing. He wrote that the discussions should focus on a goal of temporarily freezing the existing territorial control without the government, the opposition, or the Kurds giving up their arms. Additionally, measures should be agreed upon to stabilize conditions in territories controlled by these belligerents with guarantees of unrestricted access to humanitarian aid.

Secretary Blinken, what do you think about that proposal? The United States could advance that even in the absence of Russian or Syrian agreement by proposing a Chapter 7 United Nations Security Council resolution requiring all parties to immediately stop the killing, stabilize civilian populations, and ensure full access to humanitarian relief for all victims of this war. Russia's ongoing atrocious behavior in Aleppo makes it clear that they would not support such a resolution. However, it would put them on notice that at the United Nations we were about to have this global discussion of the need to just stop the killing.

Can you talk about President Carter's proposal, what you think about it, and putting aside the "Assad must go" movement for the time being so that we can just begin to put an end to this humanitarian crisis?

Mr. BLINKEN. Senator, thank you very much. And forgive me because I have not read it. So I would like to be able to read it in detail, but I heard your description of it.

First, in effect, what we have been trying to achieve, with Russia's support, is a cessation of hostilities that would, in effect, end the violence, the provision of humanitarian assistance to people who need it in besieged areas, and as I said as well, taking the Syrian air force out of the skies over civilian populated areas and getting everyone to focus on the common enemy, which is Daesh and Al Qaeda, Al Nusra, in Syria. So, in effect, those were the first steps that we thought were so critical.

Now, if we were able to take those steps, we would then have in place the conditions under which all of the parties could begin to negotiate a political transition in Syria.

Senator MARKEY. But it is broken. So what do you think about taking it to the U.N., taking it to a Chapter 7, escalating this thing to a point where everyone is going to be forced to sit down and discuss it, Syria and Russia might not like it, but at least we are going to be focusing upon the core problem of stopping the killing?

Mr. BLINKEN. So we are very actively looking at what more can be done at the United Nations.

Senator MARKEY. Would that include a Chapter 7?

Mr. BLINKEN. Sure, except that, of course, Russia would almost certainly veto a Chapter 7.

Senator MARKEY. And that is all right. Let us have Russia veto it. Let us have Russia be—let us pin the tail on the donkey. Let us have the culpable parties be put in place. Let us not allow them—I just think there is such an atmosphere of ambiguity. It is just so complex in Syria, in Aleppo. There are so many parties involved that it is just very difficult for the world to understand who has the capability——

Mr. BLINKEN. Well, you are exactly right, Senator, and that has added to the complication because we have a multiplicity of actors, all of whom have different priorities. Our priority has been in the first instance Daesh because that poses the most immediate threat to us and to our interests. Russia's priority has been to keep Assad in place or at least to maintain its foothold in Syria. The priority of the Turks has been actually dealing with the Kurds and preventing them——

Senator MARKEY. Exactly. All of that is true.

Mr. BLINKEN. The Saudis have been most interested in checking Iran.

So in all of these ways, because people come to this with different interests and different priorities, it makes it even more complicated.

That said, I think you are right that further turning up the heat at the United Nations is something that we have to very closely look at.

Senator MARKEY. The administration announced that this week it would increase the supply of arms to Kurdish militant groups in Syria to enable them to play a leading role in a future offensive to take Raqqa, a Sunni city, back from ISIS. What are the risks of relying on a Kurdish force for military operations in a Sunni Arab city? And did you discuss this with the Turkish government before you made that announcement?

Mr. BLINKEN. In fact, I was in Turkey just this week, and we are looking with our Turkish partners and allies very closely at how we continue the campaign in Syria to take territory away from Daesh.

Senator MARKEY. What was their perspective on using Kurdish troops aided by the U.S. in Raqqa?

Mr. BLINKEN. As you know, Senator, we have worked in northern Syria with something called the Syrian Democratic Forces, the SDF. That has several components. One is the Syrian Arab coalition, so predominantly Arab forces. And it also includes Kurdish forces, in this case the YPG. And the Turks have not been comfortable with support to this Kurdish element of the Syrian Democratic Forces, and it has obviously caused some tensions. But it has resulted in taking back Manbij, which was a critical transit point for Daesh in and out of Syria and in and out of Turkey. A treasure trove of information about their external plotting came from that.

And so we need to be able to work with effective actors on the ground in Syria. That is what we have done. That is what we will continue to do. But we also need to do it in a way that respects the concerns and interests of our Turkish allies. So we are in the midst of conversations with them about the best way to move forward, including on Raqqa.

Senator MARKEY. And if I could, just going back up to Mosul again in terms of your statement that it will be Sunni government officials, Sunni police that will be in charge of Mosul, does the government in Baghdad agree with that? Have they signed off on that? Are they going to keep the Shia militia out?

Mr. BLINKEN. That is their commitment, just as it is the Kurdish commitment to keep the Kurdish Peshmerga out of the city, and the core of the force that liberates Mosul will be the Iraqi Security Forces, backed by the coalition with the support of the Peshmerga. The tribal elements that are being trained, equipped, brought onboard with the goal of getting 15,000 of them will predominantly be the holding force once the city is liberated.

Senator MARKEY. Thank you, Mr. Chairman.

The CHAIRMAN. Thank you.

Our ranking member for closing comments.

Senator CARDIN. I just want to thank our Secretary for your help here. Just keep us involved on the options being considered in regards to Syria.

In regards to Mosul, it could be a wonderful advancement because militarily things look like they are in place. I share Senator

Markey's concerns that in practice we do not see the ethnic reprisals that we have seen happen so often when territory has been reclaimed from ISIS's grips. So I think that is going to be more difficult in getting the confidence necessary. So I would just urge us to work together.

In regards to Turkey, I would enjoy talking to you, not through questioning here, as to how successful we are in getting our NATO partners constructive participation in keeping the border closed but also dealing with the Kurdish issues that do not distract us from dealing with ISIS.

But I thank you very much for your service and look forward to continuing this discussion.

The CHAIRMAN. I too want to thank you for appearing today and thank you for your service and mostly for your responsiveness.

I do want to say that I think history does teach us a lot. I think basing your foreign policy on not doing what the last person did leads us to a place that is very negative for U.S. national interests. And what I hope is going to happen as people have watched the results of this strategy, is that we understand that foreign policy is much more complex—it takes more engagement than just creating a policy of not being what your predecessor was. I am hopeful that the next President and the next Secretary of State can learn from the failures that we have witnessed and hopefully in some form or capacity, what you have learned from this will be helpful in that regard as well.

Mr. BLINKEN. Mr. Chairman, I would welcome the opportunity actually to pursue that conversation at another time whenever it is convenient to you. I have to tell you from my experience we are more engaged in more places and more ways than we ever have been before. I think there is a debate about the——

The CHAIRMAN. There has been a negative trend.

Mr. BLINKEN. No. I think there is a lot of positive too, but I would be happy to pursue that conversation.

The CHAIRMAN. I would welcome that and would welcome that with Secretary Kerry and others also, which I know has been difficult to achieve.

But with that, the meeting is adjourned.

The record will remain open through the close of business Monday. If you could fairly promptly, with all the other responsibilities you have, respond to those. We thank you for being here.

The meeting is adjourned.

[Whereupon, at 11:20 a.m., the hearing was adjourned.]

ADDITIONAL MATERIAL SUBMITTED FOR THE RECORD

RESPONSES TO QUESTIONS FOR THE RECORD SUBMITTED TO DEPUTY SECRETARY BLINKEN BY SENATOR RUBIO

Question. A top IRGC commander last week said that the IRGC and its allies supply intelligence for Russia's airstrikes in Syria. Given that the IRGC and Russia are working closely in Syria, why would this administration ever agree to share intelligence and targeting priorities with the Russian military?

Answer. The United States has not been sharing intelligence information or targeting priorities with the Russian military and would never share information with Russia in support of the regime. On September 9, Secretary Kerry and Russian Foreign Minister Lavrov reached an arrangement that would have eventually resulted in the establishment of a Joint Implementation Center (JIC) for closer coordination specifically to counter al-Qaida in Syria and Daesh, which remain significant threats. The arrangement included several pre-conditions designed to test the veracity of Russia's commitments before establishing the JIC, which Russia has so far failed to honor.

Question. A press report stated that the Obama administration wired $850,000 in July 2015 to an account for Iran in the Netherlands.

- ♦ Can you confirm this wire transfer took place?
- ♦ Is it fair to say that wire transfer occurred during a period of heightened sanctions against Iran?
- ♦ Can you confirm the administration wired the $8.6 million payment to Iran for the heavy water transfer?
- ♦ Why did the President and others say that the $1.7 billion ransom payment to Iran had to be in cash because of the inability to wire money to Iran?

Answer. The July 2015 payment you are referring to was the result of an award from the Iran-U.S. Claims Tribunal at The Hague ("the Tribunal") to Iran for less than $1 million. The award was paid via wire to an account of the Iranian Center for International Legal Affairs, or CILA, in the Netherlands. CILA is the Iranian office responsible for representing Iran before the Tribunal. No direct transfer was made from the U.S. to Iran. Iran asked us to wire the award payment to that account in the Netherlands, as CILA was able to absorb the funds for purposes of paying Iran's Tribunal and litigation expenses.

As the President said, U.S. banks do not have direct banking relationships with Iran. Iran has encountered problems with a wide variety of payments prior to sanctions relief under the Joint Comprehensive Plan of Action (JCPOA) and, even after Implementation Day, prior to Iran's reconnection with SWIFT and some European banks. The payments in January 2016, which were made as part of a settlement of a long-standing claim before the Tribunal, and did not constitute a ransom payment, occurred before Iran reestablished these banking connections. The payments were structured to provide Iran access to the funds and avoid the otherwise certain delay and immobilization of the funds prior to banking reconnections, which was essential to closing the settlement agreement and saving the U.S. taxpayer potentially billions of dollars.Regarding the heavy water payment, in the months following the lifting of sanctions under the JCPOA, Iran began to gain incremental access to the international financial system, which opened up more options for executing transactions, such as the heavy water transaction you referenced. Even this transaction took several months to complete, however.

Question. Several administration officials have justified these payments to Iran coinciding with release of hostages by claiming that there were three separate negotiations happening at the same time (JCPOA implementation, release of U.S. hostages, and resolution of the Iranian claim), which naturally converged on January 17.

- ♦ If there were three separate tracks, can you confirm that three separate U.S. officials negotiated these issues in the run-up to January 17, 2016?
- ♦ Did three separate U.S. officials sign documentation on JCPOA implementation including the treatment of Bank Sepah under the JCPOA, release of the U.S. hostages, and resolution of the Iranian claim?
- ♦ If not, what U.S. official signed the bilateral documents between Iran and the United States resolving these three tracks?
- ♦ What is the name of the Iranian official who signed the documents committing to Iran's effort? What is his affiliation? What group does he work for?
- ♦ Was the transfer of the cash timed in any way to coincide with the release of the hostages?
- ♦ Given all of these facts: how was this not a ransom payment?

Answer. The President and the Secretary have made clear, the United States transferred funds to Iran to effectuate the settlement of a long-standing claim at the U.S.-Iran Claims Tribunal at The Hague. The timing of the Hague settlement was a consequence of the United States taking advantage of the opening of diplomatic opportunities with Iran on several fronts simultaneously, including the opportunity to minimize litigation risk with respect to Iran's contract claims arising under the U.S.-Iran Foreign Military Sales ("FMS") Program. Implementation Day of the Joint Comprehensive Plan of Action (JCPOA), the release of several American citizens unjustly imprisoned in Iran, and the settlement of the Hague claim were all made possible by this intensified diplomatic engagement, but all were resolved on their own merits.

Regarding the allegations that this settlement constituted ransom to free American citizens who were released from prison in Iran on January 17, the administration has repeatedly made it clear since January, and President Obama recently reiterated, that this settlement did not constitute ransom and that the United States has not and will not pay ransom. Upon Iran's release of several unjustly detained Americans, the United States provided relief to certain Iranian citizens charged with primarily sanctions-related crimes, several of whom are dual U.S.-Iranian nationals, as a one-time reciprocal humanitarian gesture.

Question. In June of this year, 51 State Department officials submitted a memo through the Department's "dissent channel" in which they called for the United States to carry out military strikes against the Assad government in order to stop its cease fire violations. They wrote that if the Obama administration continued to allow the Assad government and its backers to attack Syrian civilians with impunity, the situation in Syria will "continue to present increasingly dire, if not disastrous, humanitarian, diplomatic, and terrorism-related challenges." Do you agree with these diplomats within your Department that the failure of the administration's efforts has indeed allowed the situation Syria to deteriorate, leading to the consequences which they warned of?

Answer. There is no way to look at what is happening on the ground in Syria and not feel profound grief and horror. In the midst of such tragedy, it is tempting to want a neat answer that ends the civil war and eases suffering overnight. But the challenges before us defy silver bullet solutions. These are extremely tough issues: How to get a successful cessation of hostilities; how to ensure full, unimpeded humanitarian access to all Syrians in need; and how to bring about a genuine political transition in accordance with the Geneva Communique. We are working all-day, every day to defeat Daesh in Syria, Iraq and elsewhere. We have regular, frank discussions about how best to go about it. We are very focused on reducing the violence and providing humanitarian assistance to the still millions of Syrians in need.

We do not believe there is a military solution to this conflict, so we are working to bring about a political resolution, which includes a transition away from Assad.

Question. As Ambassador Samantha Power told the United Nations Security Council Sunday, "The Assad regime believes only in a military solution. It says it is going to conquer militarily every last square inch of Syria." And "Instead of pursuing peace, Russia and Assad make war. Instead of helping get life-saving aid to civilians, Russia and Assad are bombing the humanitarian convoys, hospitals, and first responders who are trying desperately to keep people alive." Does this behavior indicate at all that Moscow or Damascus is interested in pursuing a political transition in Syria? How would you rate the prospects of achieving any durable ceasefire agreement in the near future, in light of recent events?

Answer. We are alarmed by the devastation inflicted on Syrian civilians, most recently in Aleppo, at the hands of the Syrian regime and its allies. We regret that Damascus has not signaled a serious intent to engage in talks aimed at a political settlement to the Syrian conflict. We remain committed to pursuing a durable resolution to the conflict, including an enduring cessation of hostilities by the Syrian regime and its allies.

We know from history and experience that civil wars end in one of three ways. First, one side wins. That is unlikely in Syria because as soon as one side gets the advantage, the outside patrons of the other side intensify their engagement to right the balance.

Second, the parties exhaust themselves. Typically, that takes a decade or longer when a multiplicity of actors are involved. The civil war in Syria is entering year six, and it features a broad array of internal and external actors with different priorities.

Third and finally, civil wars end when external powers intervene either militarily or politically. But military intervention typically adds fuel to the fire, extending before ending the conflict and suffering. In the case of Syria, short of a wholesale invasion that no outside power has the interest to undertake, military intervention is not likely to be decisive. That leaves a political intervention, with key outside powers and patrons shaping, supporting and imposing a resolution. That is the effort we have been engaged in with Russia and other members of the International Syria Support Group (ISSG), building on the foundation of the Geneva communiques and U.N. Security Council resolutions.

Question. State Department spokesman Mark Toner said this week that the "diplomatic process is still the best option we have." In light of Secretary Kerry's statement Monday that "the Assad regime statements are almost meaningless at this point in time," upon what basis can the administration hope that it can negotiate Assad, Russia or Iran into limiting their slaughter of the Syrian people?

Answer. The Assad regime continues to prove that it is not a legitimate representative of the Syrian people, and its statements are almost meaningless at this point. Nevertheless, the diplomatic process known as the International Syria Support Group (ISSG) currently remains the best option for reducing violence and helping create conditions for U.N.-led intra-Syria talks on a political solution to move forward. Since the causes of the Syrian war can only be addressed through a political solution, even if we augment our efforts with elements of other options, we and our partners must continue undertaking some form of diplomacy along the lines of the ISSG process in pursuit of the goals elaborated in U.N. Security Council Resolution 2254.

Question. Would you agree that Russia was responsible for the September 19 attack on the humanitarian aid convoy and that this attack was deliberate? What evidence can you provide this committee to corroborate that?

Answer. The regime was almost certainly aware of the convoy's route, since Syrian authorities had signed facilitation letters at the urging of the International Syria Support Group (ISSG)'s Humanitarian Access Task Force, which includes Russia. As co-chair of the ISSG Ceasefire Task Force, Russia bears at least indirect responsibility for failing to prevent the regime's attack on the convoy.

Question. The Daily Beast reported earlier this week that the U.S. special envoy to Syria Michael Ratney was warned that the Assad regime was planning to attack the Aleppo facilities of the Syrian Civil Defense.

♦ Do you deny that the U.S. was warned of the pending Assad regime attack?

♦ If you knew about the attack beforehand, why did we stand by to allow the Assad regime to attack?

Answer. The September 23 attacks on the Syrian Civil Defense ("White Helmets") positions were an especially egregious example of the kind of barbarity the Assad regime has displayed over the past five years of war. There can be no excuse for bombing facilities and supplies used to help the victims of violence. No one in the U.S. government, including Special Envoy Michael Ratney, received any warning specific to the attack on the White Helmets.

Question. The New York Times reported last week that "The Obama administration is weighing a military plan to directly arm Syrian Kurdish fighters combating the Islamic State, a major policy shift that could speed up the offensive against the terrorist group but also sharply escalate tensions between Turkey and the United States."

♦ Can you confirm that the administration is indeed considering providing Kurdish forces with small arms and other equipment?

♦ How will providing these arms enable the Kurdish forces to advance against the Islamic State?

♦ Why is the administration using the Syrian Democratic Forces as its primary proxy group in the conflict? Can you estimate the breakdown of ethnic groups within the alliance?

♦ Does the administration believe that the alliance can hold territory that is liberated from ISIS? In light of the Syrian Democratic Forces' strong Kurdish element, do you believe it is wise to use this force to continue to push into territory that is traditionally not Kurdish and what is your assessment about how they will be received by the local population?

♦ How does the administration weigh the risks of further exacerbating tensions with Ankara and reclaiming territory from ISIS? Can you identify other groups in Syria at the moment that the United States can support with equal measure?

Answer. The Syrian Democratic Forces (SDF) is a multi-ethnic Syrian alliance comprising Kurdish, Arab, Turkmen, Assyrian, Christian, and Muslim groups united in their fight against Daesh. The SDF has been a proven and valuable partner in the counter-Daesh fight and has liberated 25 percent of the terrain Daesh once controlled in Syria in 2014. We are now evaluating what role the SDF can play in the next phase of the counter-Daesh campaign in Syria.

We have not, to date, provided U.S. ammunition or weapons to the Kurdish elements of the SDF under the program established by section 1209 of the National

Defense Authorization Act for Fiscal Year 2015. The Department of Defense has provided equipment to vetted Arab elements of the SDF under section 1209. This has been a valuable contribution to the counter-Daesh mission, as it supports a vetted force's efforts to secure the region from terrorist control.

From the liberation of Kobani until the liberation of Manbij, the SDF's fighting force of Kurdish, Arab, Turkmen, Assyrian, Christian, and Muslim and other populations has been essential in recapturing significant territory from Daesh and in denying Daesh access to large portions of northern Syria. I cannot go into the specifics of the composition of the SDF.

Despite mounting multiple SVBIEDs and counterattacks, Daesh has been unable to reclaim any territory lost to the SDF. A core principle of our counter-Daesh campaign in Iraq and Syria is that local forces should hold and secure terrain liberated from Daesh. We are applying this principle in Manbij, the city most recently liberated by the SDF, and we will seek to apply it in Raqqa.

Most recently, the SDF force that liberated Manbij comprised Kurdish and Arab elements, including Arab groups from Manbij. When the SDF seized central Manbij on August 12, we saw widespread jubilation among the local population. Within a day of the city's liberation, thousands of IDPs began returning to the city, and 70,000 have returned to date. While challenges persist in Manbij, local forces are providing security, people are returning, and the local economy is regenerating. Daesh will seek to generate hostility among Raqqa's population against any counter-Daesh force advancing on the city. Counteracting and mitigating the threats caused by such Daesh propaganda campaigns is key component of our plan to liberate Raqqa.

The United States remains focused on the counter-Daesh Coalition to degrade and defeat Daesh. An important part of this effort is denying Daesh access to Syria's border, to prevent attacks in Turkey, Europe, and against the Homeland. Turkey is a key partner in the counter-Daesh Coalition, and we will continue to work with Turkish officials to discuss our mutual goal of defeating Daesh and to coordinate our counter-Daesh campaign. Since August 24, the Coalition has made significant progress in driving Daesh off the border between Syria and Turkey. We are going to work with Turkey and our counter-Daesh coalition partners to focus on that fight ahead as we continue to isolate Raqqa. As we accelerate our campaign and move toward the next phase in the isolation of Raqqa, it is critical that we are closely linked with partners on the ground to coordinate both military and diplomatic efforts to sustain the positive momentum that has been gained in recent months. The coalition will work with all of our partners to achieve our common goal—the lasting defeat of Daesh.

RESPONSES TO QUESTIONS FOR THE RECORD SUBMITTED
TO DEPUTY SECRETARY BLINKEN BY SENATOR PERDUE

Question. The Wall Street Journal recently reported that Special Envoy Brett McGurk signed three documents in Geneva, Switzerland on January 17, 2016. One of these documents reportedly committed the U.S. to support the immediate sanctions delisting of two Iranian banks, Bank Sepah and Bank Sepah International, who were not to be delisted until 2023. Both of these banks were designated by Treasury in 2007 for their role in backing Iran's missile program. The designation was silent on any role the banks played on Iran's nuclear program. How do you justify the delisting of Bank Sepah and Bank Sepah international, given the administration told us that the JCPOA sanctions relief would only be related to nuclear designations? Since Special Envoy McGurk works on the Counter-ISIL portfolio, why was he the one to sign these documents with Iran? Could you provide the three documents signed on January 17, 2016 to me and my staff for review? Why were these three documents kept from Congress in the first place?

Answer. The documents you request were provided to the Senate on September 9 and are available for review by you (and your staff holding appropriate security clearances) in the Office of Senate Security.

By January 2016, the U.S. government had already made the determination that it would remove Bank Sepah from our domestic Specially Designated Nationals and Blocked Persons (SDN) list on Implementation Day—a decision that was outlined clearly in the Joint Comprehensive Plan of Action (JCPOA) itself in July 2015. We made this determination after a careful review of the activity of all individuals and entities—including Bank Sepah—that would be removed from the SDN list as part of the JCPOA.

The United Nations Security Council decided to delist Bank Sepah in January—a public act that was reported at the time. It has long been U.S. practice to support delistings at the U.N. that match up, or synchronize, the U.S. and U.N. lists. Given the U.S. government's removal of Bank Sepah from our SDN list pursuant to the JCPOA, we were comfortable with its removal from the U.N. sanctions list as well. As we have said previously, we have the ability to quickly reimpose U.S. sanctions if Bank Sepah or any other entity engages in activities that remain sanctionable.

Special Presidential Envoy McGurk served as Deputy Assistant Secretary of State for Iraq and Iran from August 2013 until November 2015 and in that capacity was asked to lead the discussions with Iran regarding unjustly detained Americans in Iran. As the Deputy Special Presidential Envoy on the Counter-Daesh campaign, he retained his position as the Deputy Assistant Secretary for Iraq and Iran. When President Obama appointed Mr. McGurk as the Special Presidential Envoy in November 2015, he continued the sensitive talks with Iran regarding the unjustly detained Americans until they were released in January 2016. He was also the senior U.S. official present in Geneva during the discussions in which a number of strands of diplomacy related to Iran were concluded with the Iranians.

Question. I have previously written to the State Department regarding the $1.7 billion in cash payments provided to Iran this year. Unfortunately, in the reply from the State Department several of my questions went unanswered. I will repeat them here, and appreciate your thorough and direct answers to these questions:

- Why did the administration not disclose information about this payment to Congress?
- Upon making this payment, did you have any monitoring systems in place for the end-use of this cash?
- Did you receive any assurances from the Iranians that this payment would not be used to fund terrorism, the Assad regime in Syria, or other Iranian efforts to further sow instability in the region?
- Can you assure us that U.S. taxpayer dollars—specifically the hard currency provided in the January 2016 shipment—have not been used to fund terrorism?

Answer. This issue of the January settlement of the Foreign Military Sales (FMS) Trust Fund claim at the Iran-U.S. Claims Tribunal was openly addressed in January 2016, including by the President and by Secretary Kerry, and the administration made multiple offers to brief Members at that time. One Member of Congress accepted the offer of a briefing, and it was provided in April.

On September 6, we provided two closed briefings on this issue to House and Senate staff, and we have made every effort to answer questions that Members have asked. For both the payments to settle the dispute (one covering principal and the other covering the compromise on interest), no direct transfer was made from any U.S. account to Iran. The transactions that were made to effectuate the payments complied with U.S. sanctions laws and did not require a unique license, waiver, or any other form of authorization. The Department of the Treasury's Iranian Transactions and Sanctions Regulations explicitly authorizes "[a]ll transactions necessary. to payments pursuant to settlement agreements entered into by the United States Government" in a legal proceeding in which the U.S. is a party, which would include settlements of claims before the Tribunal.

We have no information to indicate that the $1.7 billion went to the Islamic Revolutionary Guard Corps or was used to support terrorism. If we determine Iran has used any of its funds for purposes that are sanctionable, such as support for terrorism, we retain the ability to take aggressive steps to counter these activities using a range of tools—including with sanctions. Iran's ongoing economic difficulties make it hard to divert large portions of these settlement funds away from its domestic economy and toward its regional activities. We estimate that Iran needs about half a trillion dollars to meet pressing investment needs and government obligations and it is our assessment that Iran has used most of the funds it has gained access to since the JCPOA to address these domestic economic needs.

Question. In addition to the questions previously asked on the $1.7 billion in cash payments, I would appreciate clarification on why the administration deemed it necessary to make these payments in cash. Although President Obama stated on August 4 "the reason that we had to give them cash is precisely because we are so strict in maintaining sanctions and we do not have a banking relationship with Iran that we couldn't send them a check and we could not wire the money," we now know that on at least two different occasions the administration wired money to Tehran (July 2015 for the settlement of a claim and April 2016 for the payment for removal of excess heavy water). Why could the funds not be wired to Iran in January 2016, when wire payments were made last year?

Answer. The July 2015 payment you are referring to was the result of an award from the Iran-U.S. Claims Tribunal at The Hague ("the Tribunal") to Iran for less than $1 million. The award was paid via wire to an account of the Iranian Center for International Legal Affairs, or CILA, in the Netherlands. CILA is the Iranian office responsible for representing Iran before the Tribunal. No direct transfer was made from the U.S. to Iran. Iran asked us to wire the award payment to that account in the Netherlands, as CILA was able to absorb the funds for purposes of paying Iran's Tribunal and litigation expenses.

As the President said, U.S. banks do not have direct banking relationships with Iran. Iran has encountered problems with a wide variety of payments prior to sanctions relief under the Joint Comprehensive Plan of Action (JCPOA) and, even after Implementation Day, prior to Iran's reconnection with SWIFT and some European banks. The payments in January 2016, which were made as part of a settlement of a long-standing claim before the Tribunal occurred before Iran reestablished these banking connections. The payments were structured to provide Iran access to the funds and to avoid the otherwise certain delay and immobilization of the funds prior to banking reconnections, which was essential to closing the settlement agreement and saving the U.S. taxpayer potentially billions of dollars.

Regarding the heavy water payment, in the months following the lifting of sanctions under the JCPOA, Iran began to gain incremental access to the international financial system, which opened up more options for executing transactions, such as the heavy water transaction you referenced. Even this transaction took several months to complete, however.

Question. Secretary Kerry appeared before this committee in February and said "Assad himself is going to have to make some real decisions about the formation of a transitional governance process that's real." If he did not meet this test of facilitating a political transition, we were told there would be "Plan B options being considered." The administration did not enact a Plan B after the target date of August 1. Why did President Obama fail to enforce his own policy again? In light of the collapse of the truce, the attack on the U.N. aid convoy, and the ongoing siege of Aleppo, is the administration now conducting any discussions at all about finally enacting Plan B measures? If not, why would the administration give the Syrian people hope for 6 months that it would finally intervene on their behalf?

Answer. Since the Secretary's appearance before the committee in February, there have been two more rounds of U.N.-led talks with Syrian opposition and regime negotiators in Geneva to explore ways forward for negotiations on Syrian political transition. On February 22, the United States and Russia announced the Cessation of Hostilities (CoH). In its initial months, our approach appeared to be working as the CoH significantly reduced violence and facilitated unprecedented humanitarian access inside Syria. As the August 1 target date approached, the United States and Russia were engaged in intensive negotiations of an arrangement that would have strengthened the CoH and thereby created conditions on the ground in Syria to allow Syrian opposition to return to a fourth round talks in Geneva by or soon after the August 1. Secretary Kerry concluded that arrangement with Russian Foreign Minister Lavrov on September 9 with the intention of garnering the endorsement of the International Syria Support Group (ISSG) at the ISSG ministerial on the margins of the U.N. General Assembly meeting on September 20. Unfortunately, Russia failed to meet its commitments under the CoH and the September 9 arrangement by, among other things, failing to prevent the September 19 attack on the U.N. convoy and other acts of regime aggression in Aleppo and elsewhere in Syria. The administration is now evaluating other options.

Question. What is the United States' overall strategy toward the Syria conflict?

Answer. The United States' overall strategy toward the Syrian conflict aims to achieve three fundamental objectives: 1) defeat the Islamic State in Iraq and the Levant (ISIL), or Daesh; 2) promote Syria's peaceful democratic political transition away from the Assad regime; and 3) ease the suffering of the Syrian people. Accordingly, the United States initiated the diplomatic process known as the International Syria Support Group (ISSG) to reduce violence and help create conditions for U.N.-led intra-Syria talks on a political solution to move forward.

Unfortunately, Russia thus far has not lived up to its commitments as a co-chair of the ISSG Ceasefire Task Force to pressure the Assad regime to abide by the terms of the Cessation of Hostilities (CoH) announced by the United States and Russia on February 22, 2016, or by those of the U.S.-Russia arrangement for strengthening the COH reached by Secretary Kerry and Russian Foreign Minister Lavrov in Geneva on September 9, 2016.

Since the causes of the Syrian war can only be resolved through a political solution, even if we augment our efforts with elements of other options, we and our partners will continue to consult work together to put pressure on Russia and undertake diplomacy along the lines of the ISSG process in pursuit of the goals elaborated in U.N. Security Council Resolution 2254.

Question. Should Russia and Syria not come to the table, will the administration reconsider bolstering support for moderate opposition forces?

Answer. Should Russia and Syria not be willing to comply with their commitments under U.N. Security Council Resolution 2254 and related resolutions, the administration will evaluate a wide range of options—including various kinds of additional support to moderate opposition resisting the Assad regime to augment the non-lethal support we have provided to date. In evaluating these options, we must also consider the political-military implications for other U.S. interests inside Syria, including our campaign to defeat Daesh, as well as in neighboring countries and surrounding regions.

Question. What leverage do we have in Syria to make Russia change its calculus and considerations for supporting Assad? Could Russia have stopped Assad from intensifying the conflict, as he has done over the past few weeks?

Answer. We are continually evaluating the types of leverage available to us to persuade Russia to press the Assad regime to comply with its commitments under U.N. Security Council Resolution 2254 and related resolutions—including various kinds of additional support to moderate opposition resisting the Assad regime to augment the non-lethal support we have provided to date.

On February 22, the United States and Russia announced the Cessation of Hostilities (CoH). In its initial months, our approach appeared to be working as the CoH significantly reduced violence and facilitated unprecedented humanitarian access inside Syria—seemingly in large measure due to Russia's influence over the regime. During August and September 2016, the United States and Russia were engaged in intensive negotiations of an arrangement that would have strengthened the CoH and proven the extent of Russia's ability and willingness to restrain the regime's military, especially its air force. Secretary Kerry concluded that arrangement with Russian Foreign Minister Lavrov on September 9 with the intention of garnering the endorsement of the International Syria Support Group (ISSG) at the ISSG ministerial on the margins of the U.N. General Assembly meeting on September 20. Unfortunately, Russia failed to meet its commitments under the CoH and the September 9 arrangement by failing to prevent the September 19 attack on the U.N. convoy and other regime aggression in Aleppo and elsewhere in Syria. The administration is evaluating other options for leverage over Russia and the Assad regime. The cost of maintaining this war in support of Assad as well as its shaming by the international community is another deterrent to Russia for maintaining its destructive role in Syria. As time goes on, the costs will only increase for Russia.

Question. What leverage do we have to change the behavior of the Assad regime? Can we exert any additional pressure on the Syrian government? Is this administration willing to do so?

Answer. We are continually evaluating the types of leverage available to us to press the Assad regime to comply with its commitments under U.N. Security Council Resolution 2254 and related resolutions—including various kinds of additional support to moderate opposition resisting the Assad regime to augment the non-lethal support we have provided to date. Besides support for the moderate opposition, we have sought to bolster our leverage on the regime through the International Syria Support Group (ISSG) process, which includes Russia and Iran and more than 20 other countries and entities with influence over the parties, to focus international pressure on the regime. While the administration willing to exert additional forms of pressure, we must also consider the political-military implications for other U.S. interests inside Syria, including our campaign to defeat Daesh, as well as in neighboring countries and surrounding regions.

Question. The New York Times reported last week that "The Obama administration is weighing a military plan to directly arm Syrian Kurdish fighters combating the Islamic State, a major policy shift that could speed up the offensive against the terrorist group but also sharply escalate tensions between Turkey and the United States." Can you confirm that the administration is indeed considering providing Kurdish forces with small arms and other equipment? How will providing these arms enable the Kurdish forces to advance against the Islamic State?

Answer. The Syrian Democratic Forces (SDF) is a multi-ethnic Syrian alliance comprising Kurdish, Arab, Turkmen, Assyrian, Christian, and Muslim groups united in their fight against Daesh. The SDF has been a proven and valuable partner in the counter-Daesh fight and has liberated 25 percent of the terrain Daesh once controlled in Syria in 2014. We are now evaluating what role the SDF can play in the next phase of the counter-Daesh campaign in Syria.

In his testimony during the week of September 19, Secretary Carter noted no decisions have been made to arm Syrian Kurds to conduct counter-Daesh operations. We have not, to date, provided U.S. ammunition or weapons to the Kurdish elements of the SDF under the program established by Section 1209 of the NDAA for Fiscal Year 2015. The Department of Defense has provided equipment to vetted Arab elements of the SDF under Section 1209. This has been a valuable contribution to the counter-Daesh mission, as it supports a vetted force's efforts to secure the region from terrorist control.

Question. Why is the administration using the Syrian Democratic Forces as its primary proxy group in the conflict? Can you estimate the breakdown of ethnic groups within the alliance? Does the administration believe that the alliance can hold territory that is liberated from ISIS? In light of the Syrian Democratic Forces' strong Kurdish element, do you believe it is wise to use this force to continue to push into territory that is traditionally not Kurdish?

Answer. The Syrian Democratic Forces (SDF) have been a proven and valuable partner in the counter-Daesh fight; it a capable, resilient, and committed force and has liberated 25 percent of the terrain Daesh once controlled in Syria in 2014. From the liberation of Kobani until the liberation of Manbij, the SDF's fighting force of Kurdish, Arab, Turkmen, Assyrian, Christian, and Muslim and other populations have been essential in recapturing significant territory from Daesh and in denying Daesh access to large portions of northern Syria. I cannot go into the specifics of the composition of the SDF.

Despite mounting multiple suicide vehicle-borne improvised explosive devices (SVBIEDs) and counterattacks, Daesh has been unable to reclaim any territory lost to the SDF.

A core principle of our counter-Daesh campaign in Iraq and Syria is that local forces should hold and secure terrain liberated from Daesh. We are applying this principle in Manbij, the city most recently liberated by the SDF, and we will seek to apply it in Raqqa.

Most recently, the SDF force that liberated Manbij comprised Kurdish and Arab elements, including Arab groups from Manbij. When the SDF seized central Manbij on August 12, we saw widespread jubilation among the local population. Within a day of the city's liberation, thousands of IDPs began returning to the city and 70,000 have returned to date. While challenges persist in Manbij, local forces are providing security, people are returning, and the local economy is regenerating. Daesh will seek to generate hostility among Raqqa's population against any counter-Daesh force advancing on the city. Counteracting and mitigating the threats caused by such Daesh propaganda campaigns is key component of our plan to liberate Raqqa.

Question. How does the administration weigh the risks of further exacerbating tensions with Ankara and reclaiming territory from ISIS? Can you identify other groups in Syria at the moment that the United States can support with equal measure?

Answer. The United States remains focused on the counter-Daesh coalition to degrade and defeat Daesh. An important part of this effort is denying Daesh access to Syria's border, to prevent attacks in Turkey, Europe, and against the United States. Turkey is a key partner in the counter-Daesh coalition and we will continue to work with Turkish officials to advance our mutual goal of defeating Daesh and to coordinate our counter-Daesh campaign. Since August 24, the counter-Daesh coalition has made significant progress in driving Daesh from the border between Syria and Turkey. Recently, President Obama had the chance to discuss with President Erdogan our support for Turkey as both a NATO ally and a key partner in the fight against Daesh . Still, there are several areas in northern Syria that are deeply important to Daesh. We are going to work with Turkey and our counter-Daesh coalition partners to focus on that fight ahead as we continue to isolate Raqqa. As we accelerate our campaign and move towards the next phase in the isolation of Raqqa, it is critical that we are closely linked with partners on the ground to coordinate both military and diplomatic efforts to sustain the positive momentum that has been gained in recent months. The coalition will work with all of our partners to achieve our common goal—the defeat of Daesh.

Over the last few weeks, the counter-Daesh coalition has removed Daesh from the Syria and Turkey border. We view this effort as a critical aspect of our campaign to defeat Daesh and prevent attacks in Turkey, Europe, and the United States. Looking forward, there remain several areas near the border that must be liberated from Daesh control. To help achieve this objective and building on the air strikes we have provided thus far, U.S. special operations forces are accompanying Turkish and vetted Syrian opposition forces as they continue to clear territory from Daesh near the border. The United States will continue to support the counter-Daesh fight across northern Syria with our partners.

Question. As Ambassador Samantha Power told the UNSC on Sunday, "the Assad regime believes only in a military solution. It says it is going to conquer militarily every last square inch of Syria instead of pursuing peace, Russia and Assad make war." In light of Syria and Russia's behavior, is the administration considering a serious change to our policy towards how to end the conflict? Is a military solution being considered?

Answer. We are alarmed by the devastation inflicted on Syrian civilians, most recently in Aleppo, at the hands of the Syrian regime and its allies. We regret that Damascus has not signaled a serious intent to engage in talks aimed at a political settlement to the Syrian conflict. We remain committed to pursuing a durable resolution to the conflict, including an enduring cessation of hostilities by the Syrian regime and its allies. Russia failed to uphold its commitments under U.N. Security Council resolutions, and potentially its obligations under international humanitarian law, to ensure Syrian regime adherence to the arrangements to which Moscow agreed. We continue to press for a resolution to the Syrian conflict, including through the International Syria Support Group (ISSG).

Question. As you're aware, in June, 51 State Department officials submitted a memo through the Department's "dissent channel" in which they called for the U.S. to carry out military strikes against the Assad regime in order to stop its ceasefire violations. They wrote that if the Obama administration continued to allow the Assad government and its backers attack Syrian civilians with impunity, the situation in Syria will "continue to present increasingly dire, if not disastrous, humanitarian, diplomatic, and terrorism-related challenges." Do you agree with these diplomats within your Department that the failure of the administration's efforts has indeed allowed the situation in Syria to deteriorate, leading to the consequences they warned of?

Answer. These are extremely tough issues: How to get a successful, cessation of hostilities; how to ensure full, unimpeded humanitarian access to all Syrians in need; and how to bring about a genuine political transition in accordance with the Geneva Communique. We are also working all-day, every day to defeat Daesh in Syria, Iraq and elsewhere. We have regular, frank discussions about how best to go about it. We are very focused on reducing the violence and providing humanitarian assistance to the still millions of Syrians in need.

We do not believe there is a military solution to this conflict, so we are working to bring about a political solution, which includes a transition away from Assad.

Question. Is the administration willing to consider humanitarian no-fly zones to help stop the loss of life in Syria? If so, how would you plan to enforce it? If not, why?

Answer. Let me assure you that the entire administration is constantly evaluating the pros and cons of new strategies and policies with regards to Syria. We look for new strategies that will help us come to a political transition in Syria, but we also want to make sure that any new potential benefits outweigh any risks for the American people, particularly American lives.

I know there is deep interest in a no-fly zone and we have examined this issue and we will continue to do so, but, at this time, we do not believe the potential benefit outweighs the great risk and the resources constraints and tradeoffs involved. Any kind of zone would require dozens of American pilots and would be a huge strain on resources.

No-fly, buffer, or safe zones entail significant logistical questions about where such zones would be, how they would be protected on the ground, and what resources would be needed to ensure that we could achieve our intended objective. At this moment, we do not believe that the creation of a no-fly zone would be successful or promote a resolution of the crisis in Syria.

Question. Since the nuclear agreement, Iran has dramatically expanded its presence in Syria and increased its military cooperation with Moscow, including at one point, even allowing Russian planes to use air bases in Iran. Do you view this as a violation of UNSCR 2231? If so, what actions are being taken to punish Iran and Russia for this violation?

Answer. U.N. Security Council Resolution (UNSCR) 2231 prohibits the "supply, sale, or transfer to Iran, or for the use in or the benefit of Iran" of certain conventional arms, including combat aircraft, absent U.N. Security Council approval. We continue to call on all Member States to fully implement UNSCR 2231, including its provisions regarding arms transfers to Iran.

Russian refueling on Iranian territory raises concerns regarding its compliance with this provision. We are looking at this very carefully and we continue to gather information regarding these events. However, our most urgent concern with regard to Russia's actions in Syria is its ongoing support to the Syrian Regime and their offensive actions, particularly in Aleppo, which have been devastating to the Syrian people, and which have led us to suspend U.S. participation in bilateral channels that were established to sustain the Cessation of Hostilities.

Question. Would you agree that Iranian aid has enabled the Syrian regime to prolong the war? Can you affirm that Iran has not used any of the money it received under the JCPOA to finance its military and economic support for the Assad regime?

Answer. Nuclear-related sanctions were always intended to secure a verifiable deal that prevents Iran from obtaining a nuclear weapon. An Iran armed with a nuclear weapon would be able to project even more power in the region—that is one of the reasons a comprehensive, long-term deal that prevents Iran from acquiring a nuclear weapon makes the United States and the region safer. As a result of many years of U.S. and international sanctions, even after the lifting of nuclear-related sanctions, it is our assessment that Iran continues to prioritize its immediate economic and budgetary needs.

Iran's ongoing economic difficulties make it harder to divert large portions of its financial gains from sanctions relief away from its domestic economy and toward its regional activities. We estimate that Iran needs about half a trillion dollars to meet pressing investment needs and government obligations and it is our assessment that Iran has used most of the funds it has gained access to since the JCPOA to address these domestic economic needs.

Question. What more can we do to punish Iran for their involvement in the Syrian conflict? Are more options being pursued now to do so?

Answer. The President has asked all of the federal agencies to put forward options for how to respond to recent developments in Syria. Some of the options are familiar, some are new; we are very actively reviewing the options.

Regarding Iranian activity, we continue to work extensively with our partners to deter and detect Iranian threats in the region. We also have numerous domestic authorities—including sanctions—to counter Iran's support for terrorism or other destabilizing activities. We will continue to vigorously enforce our ongoing sanctions, including those related to Iran's support for terrorism, destabilizing activities in the region, ballistic missile development, and human rights abuses.

Question. Can you speak to what our Gulf allies are doing to assist in dealing with the refugee crisis created by the civil war in Syria and ISIS violence? What is this administration doing to encourage nations like the UAE, Saudi Arabia, or others to shoulder a greater burden with refugees or foreign aid?

Answer. Throughout the Syrian crisis, we have actively engaged our partners in the region—including those participating in the counter-Daesh coalition and International Syria Support Group (ISSG)—to request aid for Syrian refugees and other humanitarian assistance. The Kingdom of Saudi Arabia announced it has provided $100 million for Syrian refugees, raising its total aid to $780 million since 2011. The United Arab Emirates announced at the Fourth Donors Conference for Syria on February 4, 2016 that it would contribute $137 million. Qatar announced a $100 million, five-year education initiative for Syrian refugee children at the U.N. General Assembly last month and also announced that their total contribution to Syrian refugee relief totaled up to $1.6 billion. We will continue to request all of our counter-Daesh and ISSG partners jointly care for the suffering of the Syrian people.

○